Arizona Springs

The Desert's Draught

R. Eileen Moore

Arizona's Springs: The Desert's Draught introduces readers to the natural springs in our arid state. The book focuses on 65 specific springs as examples of the thousands of springs found across Arizona. As I am not a scientist, I found some of the scientific analysis in geology, biology and chemistry difficult to explain in describing how springs form and appear along with the life found in the riparian zones. Any mistakes are mine and should not be laid on the professionals that have so graciously given their time in answering my questions.

This manuscript is not intended as a guidebook to finding the springs. Check with the local office of your public lands agency for futher information. If the spring is on private land, please request permission to access the spring.

Photography / Eileen Moore, except where indicated.
Graphics / DeAnn Bergeron

Arizona's Springs: The Desert's Draught
R. Eileen Moore
Published by Morten Moore Publishing
415 E. Mohawk Dr.
Flagstaff, AZ

ISBN 978-0-9991108-6-7
Copyright 2019
All Rights Reserved to Ken & Ruth Mortenson

Arizona Springs
The Desert's Draught

*. . . on that day all the springs
of the great deep burst forth,
and the floodgates
of the heavens were opened.*
Genesis 7:11b

Contents

Foreword: Why the Springs?

Part I: Emergence

First Draught	3
Rock to Water	7
The Path of Water	26

Part II: Spring Narratives

Life Emerging	36
Manantial de Agua	47
Water by the Road	70
Nail Canyon	91
Remnant of an Ancient Sea	99
Apple Trees and Leopard Frogs	108
Raising Fish	117
Hot Water	125
The Desert Springs	145
The Hermitage	156

Part III: Seeking the Commonweal

Water Wars	169
Preservation	185
A Civilized Brawl	203

Why the Springs?

"Since the beginning of human settlement in the West, access to a dependable source of water has meant the difference between flourishing and struggling for survival in a harsh, unforgiving environment. Springs and other water sources have played a pivotal role in the establishment of human cultures by providing a focal point for hunting, sanctuary during times of drought, stopping-points on cross-country expeditions and settlement routes, and supplying irrigation water for crops.

Furthermore, desert water sources are among the most biologically diverse, productive, and threatened terrestrial ecosystems. Springs are particularly threatened by human activity. Lacking designation as either a "ground water" or "surface water," springs exist in a legal nebula—placing them in a position especially vulnerable to exploitation. Some plants and animals rely exclusively on the microclimates, nutrients, and habitat that occur at desert springs. Site protection is vital to many species' survival."

~ Arizona's Heritage Water

http://www.azheritagewaters.nau.edu

Part I

Emergence

Montezuma Well

The Desert's Draught

First Draught

"At one time our people lived in Ahagaskiaywa. This lake has no bottom and underneath the water spreads out wide. That's where people come out first.

"A long time ago there was no water in this lake. We lived in the bottom. Our chief knew his daughter was very angry at him because of his intentions toward her. When she went down to the river to think about him, a frog told her to turn into a frog like him. He told her to swallow what her father released when he came down to use the toilet. The next morning when her father appeared on the trail, she turned into a frog. Over four days she swallowed what he released. Her father became very sick. He began to bloat, to bloat all over.

"The medicine man sang the blackroot song for him. The chief became more ill. The medicine man could do nothing more. He told the chief he was going to die.

"In her anger, his daughter was going to bring a big flood. The chief did not want his people to die in the flood. He told them to cremate his body after he died. They were to pile damp earth over his ashes, particularly over his heart. Within the damp earth, they were to plant corn.

"When the corn began to grow, it grew tall along the walls of the Ahagaskiaywa. The medicine man led the people up the stalks of corn, round and round, always up. They slept among the ears. The quail and jackrabbits followed them up. The turtle come too. He not go very fast because he is short but he make it. We all make it. When we look back we see the water coming. The frog and the woman made the water come.

"Now the flood is in the Well. The water does not come out, just lays there, so smooth.

Our corn came from Ahagaskiaywa. Blue and white and red and black. These are the colors of our world. When our children are born, we go to the Well for water. We bring it back and bath them their first time. We are the Yavapai, the people of Ahagaskiaywa. This is where we come from.*

Ahagaskiaywa, the Place of Emergence

In the early morning light in late May, the water of Montezuma Well lies quiet. Ducks and mud hens lead v-shaped wakes across the surface as the sun shrinks the shadows of the surrounding walls, leaving the pool in a harsh bright light. With the temperature warming, a slight breeze begins to rise, tickling the branches of trees along the edge. Insects chirp in the underbrush.

I study the water while standing on the edge of the circular depression. The surface lies fifty-five feet below the rocky plain. The perpendicular rock walls are a light sandstone, almost as if a giant with a post hole digger has excavated an oversized pit. A narrow path drops into the well, following the ledges along the east side to a point where the water escapes under a ridge of rock.

The Yavapai people believe that Montezuma Well is the portal through which their people emerged into the present world. The comparison does not escape me. Just as a child emerges from his mother in a flood of water and blood, so the people emerged from the well into a new life. Both portals bear a circular appearance with water being released. In the origin story of this tribe the alignment between birth and emergence is obvious.

When scientists first came to the well, they could not have guessed what lay beneath the surface. In 2006, cameras were sent into the depths, sinking twenty-five, then fifty feet. At a depth of 65 feet the scientists were startled as the camera revealed undulating waves of sand as if caught in a sand storm. Downward, ever dropping, the sand increased until the camera reached a depth of 124 feet.

The water is emerging from two vents under tremendous pressure. The left vent drops sixty-nine feet, the east vent nineteen feet before becoming impassable due to the size of the fractures and the pressure of the water. This pressurized column of water and sand retains a density 1.75 times that of the water at the surface.

Year after year, for centuries, the water has continued to force its way upward under great pressure from the subterranean depths. To sustain this flow for centuries, just how much water must lie under the surface?

When the scientists spoke of the tiny cracks and the fierce flow of water that

* Adapted from Oral history of the Yavapai, Mike Harrison & John Williams, with Sigrid Khera, Edited by Carolina Butler, Acacia Publishing, 2012

resisted the intrusion of their instruments, the Yavapai laughed. Did the scientists not understand that once we emerge from the depths we cannot return?

Or, to quote a Jewish leader from the first century, "How can a man be born when he is old? Surely he cannot enter a second time into his mother's womb to be born!"

The correlation between the birth of a spring from a deep aquifer and the birth of a child is inescapable. Neither can return from whence they came. The Yavapai recognized this truth. As we consider the emergence of a spring from an arid hillside, we recognize the miraculous gift of water.

Arizona has the second highest density of springs in the contiguous 48 states. I do not have the liberty of looking at every seep and bubbling pond in the state - there are thousands upon thousands. In thinking about the springs of Arizona, let us begin by considering what a spring is, the source of the water and the types of springs we encounter in Arizona. The springs I have chosen for this discussion represent the abundance of springs in this state.

Montezuma Well, a limnocrene spring, produces 1.6 million gallons a day of water rich in carbon dioxide. The water flows under the rocky rim to emerge outside the well, flowing into Wet Beaver Creek.

The walls of Oak Creek Canyon are sandstone, a rock that serves as a aquifer, retaining the water that falls on the Coconino Plateau.

Rock To Water

To understand how a spring develops, we look to the rocks beneath our feet. Rock seems hard and invincible. When searching for water, the type of rock we encounter is important.

Take a moment to examine a rock, just pick one up from the ground. Look, not at the color, but at the granular structure. If you live in Sedona, there is a good chance that you picked up sandstone. Rubbing the stone between your fingers, the rock may feel gritty.

Sandstone has a granular structure due to each particle of sand retaining a surface with geometric planes. The minute space between the grains is filled with silica or calcium carbonite. Like sandstone, limestone also has a granular structure, the grains being coral and shell glued together by calcium carbonite.

Both sandstone and limestone can retain water within the structure of the rock. Water with an acidic ph dissolves the 'cement' that holds the grains together. As the cement dissolves, the water slides through these grains, creating channels for the water. These channels may grow into large cavities, capable of holding great amounts of water. Pools of water may even accumulate within the largest fractures.

By contrast volcanic rock shows a fine grain structure that may not be visible to the naked eye. A high degree of heat, whether subsurface or through volcanic eruption, has melted or reduced the granular structure. Volcanic rock tends to be impervious to water. As the rock cracks from tension in the earth's surface, water descends through cracks in the igneous layer, giving it a low secondary permeability. Throughout the southwest igneous caps protect large sandstone monuments from erosion.

The earth under our feet is composed of layers of rock. Shallow seas formed layers of sandstone and limestone. Volcanic activity intruded through sedimentary layers to deposit layers of igneous rock. Within these layers we find a third type of rock: aggregate heated and hardened by pressure deep within the earth and then pushed upward. Schist and slate as found in the Tapeats formation in the Grand Canyon geologic column is a metamorphic rock formed deep under the surface. Some of the mountain ranges in southern Arizona show a metamorphic core with more recent volcanic action intruding up through the older rock.

All of these layers are fractured by pressure from shifting plates deep under the earth's surface. As the rock layers shift, fault lines open, shifting the rock into a scrambled puzzle of interlocking layers. Geologists work to decode this puzzle and learn the geologic activity that has taken place over the centuries.

Turning back to the discussion of water, rain falls on the earth's surface and sinks into the soil. The water percolates into the layers of pervious rock until it reaches an underlying layer of fine-grained impervious rock. The impervious rock serves as a dam holding the water in place in the overlying sedimentary layer.

Sedimentary rock has a high water-holding capacity. Drilling rigs sink metal bits deep below the surface of the earth into the sedimentary layers. When the bit reaches a porous layer of rock, water begins to flow into the shaft created by the drilling rig. If the water burst upward from deep pressure rather than filling the bottom of the shaft, the drill rig has created an artesian well.

The aquifers held in sedimentary rock are the source of natural springs. The water, held captive, finds an outlet along a fracture in the rock and begins to move toward the surface of the earth.

Learning the composition of the rocks assists us in understanding where a spring is most likely to be found. Take a look at the geologic column for Flagstaff. In some areas, the top layer is volcanic, a relatively recent addition to our landscape. Some of Flagstaff's volcanoes were active as little as 1,000 years ago.

Beneath the volcanic deposits is a layer of red Moenkopi sandstone. The layers of volcanic rock and sandstone are not uniform in their elevation. Two major faults have resettled the rock layers south and east of Flagstaff, revealing pockets of pale Kaibab limestone underlying the Moenkopi and Toroweap formation.

The Moenkopi sandstone held shallow aquifers that early settlers accessed with their wells. The water is held in the sandstone by an underlying layer of gypsum and shale identified as the Toroweap formation.

How are aquifers recharged?

* Precipitation as rain or snow. Only about 5% of what falls actually reaches the aquifer.

*Streams and wetlands allow water to seep into the earth as do fractures in the rock.

* Effluent, the water that has been used, purified and released.

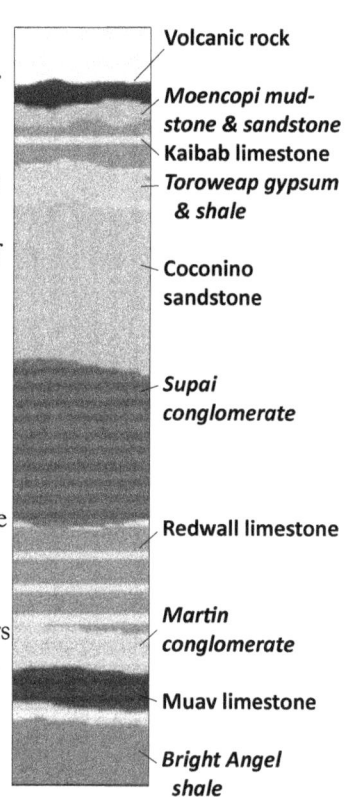

Volcanic rock

Moencopi mudstone & sandstone

Kaibab limestone

Toroweap gypsum & shale

Coconino sandstone

Supai conglomerate

Redwall limestone

Martin conglomerate

Muav limestone

Bright Angel shale

This formation is less pervious and overlays the Coconino sandstone. A cross-cut of both the Kaibab limestone and the Coconino sandstone are visible in the cliffs that line Oak Creek Canyon. The Coconino sandstone holds a lot of water that percolates down from the surface of the Coconino Plateau. This is the source of the Coconino aquifer spread across 21,655 miles under portions of four western states. The western edge lies in the Little Colorado basin, the eastern edge in New Mexico. The water within the aquifer is flowing away from the Mogollon rim in a northern to northwestern direction.

Along with many small towns across the Colorado Plateau, the city of Flagstaff draws much of its water from the Coconino aquifer. As demand increases the aquifer level is dropping. The city's well field must now draw water from the 1,200 to 1,600 foot depth. In other locations, the aquifer is closer to the surface. This difference reflects the geological formations underground causing the aquifer to vary in depth.

Successive formations of pervious rock underlie the Coconino sandstone. Around 2,700 feet above sea level, water seeping down through the rocks reaches Muav limestone which overlays the Bright Angel Shale. Shale is fine-grained and prevents much of the water that has reached the Muav limestone from going much deeper. This is important as some of the largest springs in Arizona flow from the Muav limestone.

The Coconino is not the only aquifer found in Northern Arizona. Moving into the northeast corner of the state, we come across the Navajo and the Dakota aquifers. The Navajo aquifer is located in the Navajo and Wingate sandstone while the Dakota is in a formation consisting of the Dakota, Cow Springs and Entrada sandstone.

The Navajo aquifer spreads over 6,250 square miles, north of the Little Colorado River and is the primary water source for much of the western region of the Navajo Nation. The Dakota aquifer, the smallest of the three lies along the slope of Black Mesa, east of Tuba City, covering 3,125 square miles. On the eastern edge of Arizona, along the I-40 corridor, some of the wells are drawing water from the Bidahochi formation, a shallow aquifer found in a highly eroded sedimentary layer. These aquifers are under heavy demand.

Unlike the uplift of the Colorado Plateau, the terrain of southern Arizona is dominated by isolated mountain ranges divided by deep basins. The ranges were formed by either volcanic activity or subsurface pressure. Over the centuries, large quantities of sand and rock have washed down the slopes of the mountain ranges into deep basins surrounding the ranges. Based on core samples, scientists tell us these alluvial deposits are thousands of feet deep. The sand and grit in the alluvial deposits serves as a reservoir, retaining the water and creating aquifers. Both Phoenix and Tucson utilizes these aquifers as part of their water supply. As our population grows, these aquifers are under increasing pressure to supply more water.

In the peaks above the desert plain, we also see shallow aquifers form in alluvial pockets within the folds of the terrain. These are called perched aquifers and are often the source of seasonal springs. Hydrologists suggest some of the water caught in these pockets may descend to the deeper aquifers.

Looking at a map of Arizona, we see the highest density of springs along the transitional zone between the Colorado Plateau and the Range and Basin topgraphy of the southern deserts. The Grand Canyon with its exposed layers of sedimentary rock and limestone karsts is also a hotbed of spring activity. These regions show catastophic geologic activity. We could say the springs are born in stress and fracture.

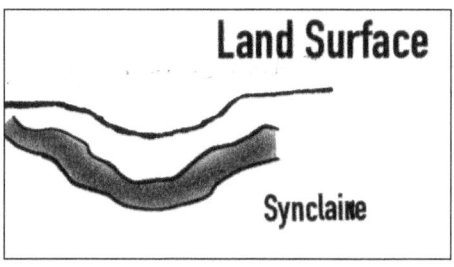

Water collects in a depression on the earth's surface due to the sycline below.

The water from these aquifers might have remained hidden underground if not for the shifting of the earth's surface. A spring develops when water caught in the sedimentary rocks finds a path to the surface along cracks in the rock created by either volcanic activity or seismic disruption. Consider three ways in which water might reach the surface along a crack.

The most basic conduit is one formed by a depression in the earth surface with the

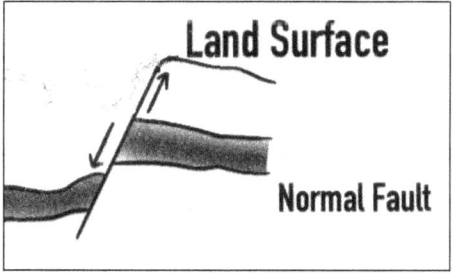

A fracture has broken the rock and pushed a layer of sedimentary rock up to the surface where it is exposed and begins to release water onto the earth's surface.

water table revealed on the ground's surface.

A second formation known as a *gravity or contact spring* emerges in several different presentations. Water seeps through layers of rock to a sedimentary layer which is eroded along a cut in the earth's surface.

A *fracture spring* is related to displacement between layers of rock. As pressure is released between the subterranean plates deep beneath the surface, the rock layers must adjust. Massive sections of rock are tilted or forced to slide against other huge sections of rock forming a *fault*. The result may be a visibly dramatic like the Mogollon Rim or more subtle like a shallow valley. Some of these faults like the Grand Wash fault in the Arizona Strip run for hundreds of miles. When a fault passes through sedimentary rock, it may present a channel for water to reach the surface.

Classifying the Springs

For those who seek out the springs, it becomes evident that not every spring emerges in the same pattern. In an effort to distinguish the types of springs, Dr. Larry Stevens of the Springs Institute at the Museum of Northern Arizona and Dr. Abraham Springer, a hydro-geologist and professor with the University of Northern Arizona, developed a classification system to identify the springs within two catagories: *Lotic* and *Lentic* springs. A Lentic spring is defined as a spring with water that does not move away from the point of emergence. In contrast, a Lotic spring moves away from the point of emergence.

Each of these two broad categories are broken into six individual types of springs. Within the *Lotic*, are the cave spring, the geyser, the gushet, the hillslope, the hanging gardens and the rheocrene springs. Of the Lotic springs, only the geyser is not found in Arizona. The *Lentic* springs include the exposure spring, the helocrene, the hypocrene, the limnocrene, the mound-forming and the fountain. The last of these, the fountain, is not found in Arizona. Many springs share more than one set of markers for classification. With this in mind, let's take a look at each type of spring, starting in the Lentic with the exposure spring.

> Arizona, the second driest state, has the second highest density of springs within the 48 contiguous states. There are around 5,000 in the Grand Canyon alone We cannot profile every spring. We have chosen about 65 springs to represent those found across Arizona.

Julia Fonseca, with the Pima County Office for Sustainability, identifies the Santa Cruz River in Tucson as an *exposure spring*. I was surprised as the characteristics of a river seem completely different from a contained outlet for water rising to the surface.

She explained that we see the river bed with water in a contained stretch, no water flowing from upstream into the pools, no water flowing downstream away from the pools. I asked whether this was just a sign that the river was drying up but Julia insisted that this is an exposure spring with the water table exposed within the river bed. In the early 1900s, water did emerge at the base of Sentinel Creek where the watercourse had reached bedrock, exposing the water table.

Today, some water may emerge in the creekbed north of Tucson. At least that was the only site until recently. Due to water deposits from the Central Arizona Project, the aquifer has risen over the last couple of years to now emerge along the Santa Cruz in the river bed crossing the San Xavier Pima Reservation. .

Exposure springs may be hard to recognize, sometimes being found in a cavity or sinkhole that is filled with water. The water does not flow out of the cavity but remains at a fairly consistent level.

Three Forks, a fen located above 7,000 feet elevation.

A *helocrene spring* is a spring-fed meadow. The ground surface may be a bit marshy with small pockets of water. When the Spanish entered the southwest they called the helocrene springs *cienegas*, a word we find in common usage throughout Arizona. If the cienega is located above 7,000 feet elevation, then it is called a *fen*. In crossing a fen, the ground seems to suck at one's feet with each step. Our footprints may fill as there is water hidden just below the surface.

John Reece, the hydrologist with the Apache-Springerville National Forest, insists that the region known as Three Forks could be classified as a fen. The Black River flows through thick clumps of willows dotted with ponderosa pine, passing under Forest Road 249 into meadows with thick, deep grass. One of the markers of a helocrene springs is a low gradient or slope that allows the water

One of the springs emerging from the fen.

to slow and inundate the surface of the ground. As we walked across the meadows, it seemed as if the ground was saturated with water, held in place by the rank grass.

Further on, at a point where the creek took a sharp left turn at the canyon wall is another spring that has been found to contain tiny spring-snails. Mountain sheep may be found descending the steep hillsides to the meadows and the Black River during the quiet months of the year. Both springsnail and sheep depend on the water that winds through the steep canyon walls. The springs seem to weep within these meadows as a release for the water held captive below. Unlike the helocrene, the *hypocrene* spring is a spring with water close to the surface but not visible above the

Hypocrene spring: Walk through the grass and part the long stems, looking closely at the ground underfoot. It is wet! No water is evident above ground but just below the surface a deep up-welling nourishes the tall grasses.

ground. The presence of the spring is marked by healthy vegetation on the surface. Evidence of a hypocrene spring might be a lush meadow caught in a pocket like the one shown where the water is released through the grass as transpiration.

Big Spring, a limocrene spring in Pinetop-Lakeside

Montezuma Well is an unusual example of a *limnocrene spring as* the water lies within the near vertical walls of a collapsed cavern. The water would rise to overflow the rim if not for an outlet hidden beneath the surrounding wall releasing 1100 gallons of water per minute down the slope into Wet Beaver Creek. Visitors follow a paved path toward the creek to the point where the water emerges from under the wall into a rock-lined channel.

The Well has a high concentration of dissolved carbon dioxide and arsenic. Despite the arsenic which we would consider poisonous, four species have adapted to the toxic brew: a springsnail, a leech, water scorpions and an amphipod.

Another limnocrene spring more consistent with the standard presentation is Big Spring in Pinetop-Lakeside in the White Mountains. The watershed creating this spring is relatively small at 1,500 square acres. The spring emerges at the bottom of a large pool lined with rushes. A visitor might glimpse small bubbles appearing on the pond's surface when the inflow is heavy.

The landscape around the spring shows evidence of human habitation stretching back over the centuries. A small pit house has been excavated indicating early native people lived near the spring. Early settlers were quick to identify four springs within the watershed and determined that this was a good location for settlement.

Sipapuni is an excellent example of a *mound spring*. The highly mineralized spring is found in the depths of the steep-walled canyon of the Little Colorado

Sipapuni spring, a mound spring in the Little Colorado River drainage. Photo: Bob Bordasch

River. As it emerges, the water deposits minerals around the outlet and over the years, the mineral deposit have formed a mound around the outlet. The water cascades from the outlet at the top of the mound to the base where it flows into the Little Colorado River.

Sipapuni is considered sacred ground by the Hopi and other tribes, with some clans considering this their point of emergence into the present world. The Hopi request that hikers not ascend the mound when hiking through the narrow canyon. Most of the springs in Arizona are considered sacred by native peoples and we approach each spring with respect for their beliefs and for the gift of water.

Turning to the Lotic springs, the *cave spring* flows, as one would guess, out of a cave. One such spring was found in Oak Creek Canyon in what is now Cave Spring campground. Approaching the entrance, the cleft appears as a rock vault, drawing visitors into the depths. However, visitors do not get far, finding a brick wall across the cavity just inside the entrance. Over the years vandalism had taken a toll and despite signed requests that the cave be treated with respect, the vandalism continued.

The water flowed from the rock face into a channel that led to Oak Creek. The water from Oak Creek was once channeled to homesteads and orchards in

Pivot Rock, a cave spring extends back about 65 feet into a limestone formation.

the late 1800's. In the early 1900s, George Babbitt Jr. built a home with a large pool near the cave's entrance. While he remained a bachelor throughout his life, he enjoyed allowing family and local residents to swim in the pool and explore the creek flowing through his property.

Another cave spring emerges near Pivot Rock in a narrow canyon south of Winslow. The cave entrance seems to open as a mouth cut into the hillside, sheltered by a protruding rock lip. This cave could be part of a karst system and is responsive to snow melt and precipitation. At times only a trickle can be found along the cave floor. Those few who crawl into the cave report the passage narrowing to a point where one can not proceed further. The passage is reported to split with an upper chamber that forms a balcony overlooking the passage below.

The *gushet spring* as its name indicates gushes from fracture in a rock cliff. Some of Arizona's largest and most remote springs are gushet springs. The volume and force of the water from a gushet tends to indicate that the spring is supported by a large aquifer and in some cases the aquifer may be under pressure between opposing rock layers.

A team of researchers has entered the Roaring Springs Cavern, proceeding well beyond a mile into the pitch-black passage with only headlights for illumination. Imagine, wading into the current, pushing forward, hoping not to step

Veit spring, is found on west side of the San Francisco Peaks, emerging from a basalt cliff above a deep bed of volcanic cinders. Petroglyphs appear on the cliff face created by a prehistoric people. A wavy line over the entrance seems to indicate 'Here is water.'

The spring was homesteaded by George Veit, a German emigrant. His cabin has been moved but two spring houses remain over channels below the spring. A small tank may have once provided water for the herds of sheep.

Much higher on the slopes, Basque sheep herders favored Philomena, a hillside spring above the treeline. The spring was named after the wife of one of the Babbitt brothers, merchants who sold supplies to the sheepherders. The Basque built large wooden tubs nestled in the aspen grove to store and release water into a wooden trough for their sheep. Those with a good set of lungs can climb to both springs. Looking carefully, visitors may find one of the wood tubs. Please leave this piece of northland history as you found it.

A petroglyph with wavy lines seems to indicate a source of water below.

Roaring Springs, North Rim of the Grand Canyon

Labels on image:
- Cave – point of spring emergence
- Sprayzone – the forces of the water sprays beyond the rock surface
- Malicolous – a thin sheet of water covers the rock face.
- Backwall – the water has undercut the rock ledge, leaving an alcove behind the flow.
- Terrace – the water has worn the rock face, creating ledges over which the water flows.
- Pool

Roaring Spring is more than a stream of water falling down a cliff. The riparian zone below the cave outlet is divided into zones, each with forms of life particular to that zone. Some of the species found along Arizona's springs can not be found any place else in Arizona.

into a deep crevasse. The water is icy with temperatures around 52 degrees.

Thunder River, one of the largest gushets, roars out of a fracture high on a rock cliff to create a river flowing several miles down to the Colorado River. This gushet flows from the thick layer of Muav limestone. Water percolates through the layers of Coconino sandstone and Redwall limestone to saturate the Muav limestone on the north rim of the Grand Canyon. However, it is the Bright Angel shale, an impervious layer, that holds the water within the Muav.

Most of the small springs found across Arizona are *hillslope springs*, meaning that a small outlet releases water across a hillside. The hillslope springs are often the release point, with or without a focused flow, for small perched aquifers that appear intermittantly rather than year round. One of the largest perennial hillslope springs in Arizona is east of Payson.

Horton Spring

Horton spring emerges from multiple fracture points to tumble down a rocky hillside as Horton Creek. The creek drops quickly in elevation through small cataracts and pools to disappear into the sand above the Tonto Creek drainage. Moss, algae and watercress grow along the stream's banks. A visitor descending along the creek finds a rich riparian zone with insect life feeding fish and birds. Many of the four-legged species of Arizona's mammals live within the easy reach of the creek.

Standing on the ridge above the spring, we easily observe the source of the water in the 2,000 foot cliffs of the Mogollon Rim overhead.

The *hanging garden or dripping spring* sounds like something out of a landscape architect's dream. Most hanging gardens are small seeps with a limited flow, sometimes measured at a few drops in a minute. I am most intrigued by the hanging gardens that emerge from an overhang in a rocky alcove on the North

Cliff Spring, North Rim of the Grand Canyon; moss growing in fracture rock

rim of the Grand Canyon. A short trail takes visitors from a view of the spectacular Angel's Window into a narrow canyon. Before reaching a dead-end, visitors come to Cliff Spring, an alcove beneath an overhanging rock ledge. Water drips from fractures into pools below. The pools, only an inch or so deep, are a mosaic of pockets of water, mud and human footprints overlying wildlife tracks between the green sheen of algae and moss. These springs are often found in the fractures of a sheered cliff.

Dripping springs do not have the spectacular presentation of the gushet spring, yet they are a primary source of water for wildlife across the state. The source of water may be a perched aquifers or small pockets in the rock walls. Looking overhead, we find delicate maidenhair fern, monkey flower and moss clinging to the fractures of the rock face. Small insects buzz around the cracks, for they need moisture too. In the quiet as dusk settles across the lands, when no humans intrude, small animals creep out of the shadows to sip the moisture in shallow puddles at the base of the rock.

Rheocrene springs rise along a creek bed, leaving water within the channel and contributing to the flow of runoff from rain and snow melt. For hikers arriving above the pools of water in Fossil Creek, the sudden appearance of water can be a bit disconcerting as the source is not immediately apparent. Within a few

A rheocrene spring, near Lake Mary in northern Arizona

yards downstream, the volume of water increases and in one location appears to bubble above the surface of the creek, pushed upward from pressure below. The spring backs up the channel as well as flowing downstream.

Fossil Creek is caught in a deep canyon between the Cimarron Hills and Deadman Mesa. Following the winding road that crosses the canyon, visitors gaze up at the rock layers of the mesa that contain the aquifer that feeds these springs. Dropping into the canyon from a trailhead near Payson, hikers discover lovely, clear pools of water connected by a current-rippled stream.

Along a 1,000 foot length of Fossil Creek 115 springs produce 45 cubic feet of water per second. To help put this in perspective, imagine one cubic feet as about the size of an NBA regulation basketball. Now imagine 45 basketballs crowding into the streambed every second. These are the springs of Fossil Creek. Awesome!

The water pours down the watercourse with a depth that defies one's ability to grasp the amount of water appearing in a desert climate. Standing above the

Trail entering Fossil Creek

largest waterfall, I looked upstream at a pool that seemed to rumble with the current sweeping along the pale stone walls. The torrent swept around the pool before passing over a waterfall. Below the falls, the current passes along a millrace down the stream bed. Behind the falls the water has cut a shallow cave, inviting visitors to swim through the curtain of water onto a rock shelf.

The number of large springs that emerge along the Verde Valley and the amount of water the springs produce is incredible. Much of the water has descended from the region wouth of Flagstaff on the Mogollon rim to emerge from a thick layer of limestone deep below the Valley. As with much of Arizona the Verde Valley is riven with faults that create conduits to the surface for the fractures in the sedimentary rock.

Fossil Creek rises from the junction of two faults. As water flows along the Fossil Creek fault, the Diamond Rim fault blocks its passage and forces the water to the surface. The water has a high concentration of CO_2 and dissolved carbonate which builds the travertine rock found around so many of the springs in central Arizona.

Human impact along this creek has become significant. In 1908, a power plant was built along the banks of the Verde River. A metal flume carried water from a dam built across Fossil Creek. The flume snaked down the hillside to empty into a small lake. From the lake the water flowed through pipelines and tunnnels to one small power plant from which it was flushed into the Verde River.

The flume removed much of the water that once nourished the riparian zone extending for miles along the stream bed. Environmentalists longed to see the creek returned to a natural state. Pressure was placed on Arizona Public Service which ultimately decommissioned and removed the one-megawatt plant. To their credit, the company would become an enthusiastic partner in the restoration of the stream. Restoration efforts transformed Fossil Creek into one of the jewels of the back country of Arizona.

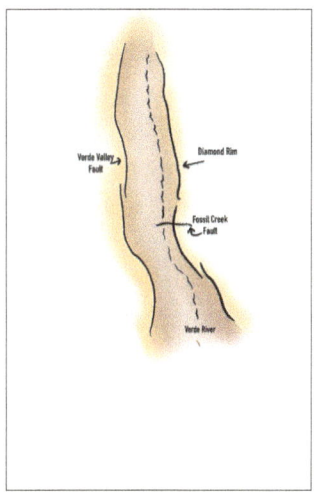

Unfortunately, as news of the beautiful stream reached the million plus people living in the urban center in the Valley of the Sun, thousands poured into the canyon to enjoy the cool, green-tinted water. The onslaught presented a new threat to the watercourse and regulations were put in place to control the number of people who could enter the canyon. Fossil Creek presents an example of the silent desire of desert dwellers to reconnect with natural sources of water.

As we think about the gift of water emerging from the earth, we can appreciate the mystical sense of awe the native tribes hold for the springs. For the native people, the springs are sacred. As such, we understand that when we visit a spring, we approach it with respect. We speak quietly and move carefully, aware that we are not the only living beings to appreciate this gift. We might sit and observe the life around the spring and listen to the buzz of insects around the moisture.

A rheocrene spring rising midstream.

One evening, I listened to author Craig Childs describe a multi-day hiking venture with a friend in the back country. They intended to explore a large red-rock gushet. Craig described days of walking across sun-blasted wilderness before reaching a vertical cliff. High overhead, water gushed from the cliff face. The men donned wet suits, knowing the water would be icy as it flowed from deep in the earth.

Climbing the vertical face of the cliff, they swung into the passage, wading into the icy stream. Their feet gripped the dimpled surface of the rock, hands flexing against the wall on either side to assist their progress. The light from the cave opening receded as Craig and his partner moved deeper into the passage with only a headlight to reveal what lay ahead.

He described his wonder as they emerged into a large cavern with inky black pools of water at their feet. His headlight caught the deepest blackish-blue glint in a ripple on the surface of a pool stretching beyond their headlamps. They could not leave without moving further into the cave. Cautiously they launched into the pools, stoking through the water to reach a large boulder that emerged from under the surface. The cold seeped through their wet suits and they knew the visit to the subterranean chamber would not last long. In those few short moments, Craig sat on his perch with the darkness threatening to engulf him at every angle. He marveled at the aquifer releasing its liquid treasure hour by hour, day after day, longer than men have kept a written record of their exploration into our western lands.

We know so little of the aquifers hidden from our sight. The springs are their calling cards, speaking of more than we can witness with our five senses. We do well to approach a spring quietly, watching and listening

More Than Rain?

Some scientists have proposed that our aquifers could be the remnants of water left from the great ice age that may have extended into the southwest. Others have laid out the proposed boundaries of an ancient lake or inland sea that once covered much of northeastern Arizona which saturated the sandstone layers with water.

I am caught by the idea that almost every tribe has a story of a great flood within its oral history. In the Biblical book of Genesis, the seventh chapter describes the beginning of this world-wide flood:

"On that day all the springs of the great deep burst forth, and the floodgates of the heavens opened. And rain fell on the earth forty days and forty nights."

Later the same chapter records the depth of the flood as covering the mountains "more than twenty feet."

Imagine that much water! This wasn't just rain but a cataclysmic event commemorated in the oral history of almost every tribe. What would have been the impact on the earth's crust? As the flood waters began to recede, where did the water go? Think of the swirling sediment. Undoubtably great layers of sediment would have been laid across the surface of metamorphic rock and saturated with water.

Is it possible that some of the water we raise to the surface is an ancient deposit from a great flood? When scientists tap some of the deeper aquifers, the water is highly mineralized. Some aquifers have been conservatively dated older than 20,000 years. We are tapping these aquifers. Is the water being replaced at a rate that can be sustained? Will the water we withdraw be replaced in our lifetime? If we consider historic accounts, the southwest region seems to be drying out. Many of the historic springs have stopped flowing, some have disappeared.

According to the Springs Institute, the total amount of freshwater on earth adds up to 22,230 cubic feet of water which equals 1/150 of the total amount of water on earth. With a finite amount of fresh water, at some point we will be required to consider whether we are using water indiscriminately. The springs, as a source of fresh water, whether ancient or yesterday's rainfall, deserve our respect and our care.

The Path of Water

We've looked at the formation of a spring and the different presentations of the springs as they appear on the surface. But where does the water come from?

We understand that water falls on the earth in the form of rain or snow. This moisture sinks into the ground but we have little idea of how long it takes for the water to collect in the aquifers or how much water is actually stored in the layers of rock. Water from some springs is clear and good tasting while other springs carry a load of minerals that leave a bad taste. Just the name *Sulfur Springs* warns that the water may be tainted. If the water entered the rock from rain and snow, how did it become so bitter?

Looking beyond the natural flow of the springs, conservationists have asked whether we are drawing more water from these aquifers than the earth can sustain. How do scientists discover the origins of the water and learn more of this cycle? How do they measure the quantities of water that may be stored in the aquifers?

This is where the hydrogeologist steps in the spotlight.

Hydrogeologists learn a great deal about the surface of the earth by studying the layers that are exposed in the Grand Canyon and other locations where deep cuts occur in the surface. In the exploration for oil and gas, high pressure drills bore into the earth's surface over 40,000 feet deep, bringing core samples to the surface. The core samples give scientists a glimpse of rock layers under our feet. The rock fround in caves and deep mines also contribute to our knowledge of the earth's crust.

Along with core samples, scientists use seismic, electro-magnetic and radar technology to study the layers of rock. Seismic tests use vibrations from a small explosive to indicate the composition of the the rock layers. The flow of an electrical current allows geologists to map fractures in the rock. A type of radar, abbreviated SAR, allows a geologist to map the surface of the earth as they study broad regions and changes to the earth's surface.

The springs also give us an understanding of the composition of what lies below the earth's surface. When hydrogeologists analyze a sample of water, they find specific combinations of atoms, known as isotopes. Water is composed of oxygen and hydrogen atoms and may be identified as rain water, snow melt or sea water. Each of these has a different isotope identified by the atom and the number of neutrons.

One of the telling signatures in a sample is the presence of tritium, a radioactive element dating back to the nuclear tests of the 1950's in the state of Nevada. If a sample of water contains tritium, then a hydrologist understands that this water that has entered the ground since the 1950's. Water prior to the 1950's does not contain tritium.

By analyzing the isotopes within a sample of water scientists, can learn the approximate age of the water sample and the path it has traveled, both vertically and laterally. As an example, many of the springs in Arizona contain calcium carbonate ($CaCO_3$), indicating the water has traveled through sedimentary rock.

Consider for a moment the water that falls near Flagstaff. Dr. Abe Springer, a hydrogeologist from Northern Arizona University, began by identifying the isotopes in the precipitation that fell around Flagstaff. He then took samples from the springs within the region surrounding Flagstaff. Based on his studies of isotope signatures, he learned that the rain that falls north of Interstate 40 near Flagstaff has the same signature as the water flowing from Blue Springs along the Little Colorado River. Hydrogeologists concluded that the Coconino aquifer flows in a north to north-west direction toward the Little Colorado River.

To drive such a distance would take a couple of hours followed by a steep plunge over the canyon's edge. One tiny snowflake, melted into fractured rock to joins millions of other drops of water following a line of fractures to emerge miles away from where it first fell to earth. This gives us a new respect for that snowball we form as we contemplate our nearest target.

Hydrogeologists found that the water flowing from Page Springs near Cottonwood, below the Mogollon Rim, also originated on the Coconino Plateau south of Interstate 40. The study of isotopes showed the water around Flagstaff emerged at two different points, 100 miles apart in opposite directions.

In a recent study on the North rim of the Grand Canyon, hydrologists Alex Wood and Benjamin Tobin along with Dr. Abraham Springer conducted studies of the springs on the Kaibab Plateau. As part of the study, they examined the layers of rock exposed on rock faces above the springs. They sampled 22 springs over 16 site visits, taking samples from each spring on at least seven different visits.

The north rim of the Grand Canyon is covered with lush green forests riven by narrow steep-walled canyons. When examining the geologic column, the uppermost layer is Coconino sandstone. This overlies a layer of Hermit shale, followed by the Supai group, a formation consisting of sandstone, siltstone and shale. Beneath these layers is the Redwall limestone which overlays the Muav limestone. Both of these limestone layers are heavily fractured. As water with an acidic ph penetrates the limestone, calcite, the glue between the grains of sand dissolves, allowing fractures within the rock to grow larger. Large cavities have formed along the interconnecting fractures. This network of fractures is called a limestone karst and a karst holds a lot of water.

The three scientists sought to determine whether the rain and snow that fell on the rim descended directly to an aquifer and remained. Or did the water travel laterally to the springs that emerge below the rim of the Grand Canyon?

Using the stable isotope found in Delta O18 and Delta D (deuterium), their analysis showed that the snow that fell in the central region of the plateau descended to the aquifer. The North Rim aquifer receives most of its water around Demotte Park, an area with extensive meadows. This region then become really important as the point of recharge for the aquifer.

However, the study also showed that the water did not remain under Demotte Park. Initially, it was believed that water descending into the rock layers did not move very far in a horizontal direction but remained beneath the point of submergence. Using a geochemical analysis of the samples taken from the Redwall springs, they found the water contained calcium, sodium chloride and sulphate. These chemicals are generally found in sedimentary layers, indicating that the water passed through the Coconino sandstone and down to the Redwall formation. As the men studied the samples, the elements and the geological column, they understood the water had traveled laterally through the rock layers to emerge at springs along the canyon wall.

The North Rim, of the Grand Canyon descends from Demotte Park toward the Rainbow Rim, forming a series of steps due to the faults in the region. The hydrologists found that some springs along these steps, like Mangum, had higher sulfate levels while the springs along the Rainbow Rim showed high levels of calcium. This further defined the passage the samples had taken through the rock layers.

Part of the tests they ran included placing a dye sample into a select number of the 7,000 sinkholes that dot the Kaibab Plateau and the North Rim of the Canyon. Not all the sinkholes were eligible as some are lined with clay, preventing water from percolating into the rock.

Researchers then checked the springs under study, analyzing the water that ran from the springs. They thought they might discover which area of the rim contributed to the water flowing from Roaring Springs. It would be logical to assume that the water flowing from this spring would come from a sinkhole located directly above the spring. This proved to be incorrect. Instead, traces of the dye showed up at Vaseys Paradise and miles downstream at Thunder River.

Returning to my initial question: Where does the water come from? The precipitation that sinks into the earth is stored in rock fractures as an aquifer until it is released through a spring or a well.

The Virgin River is a riparian zone, winding through dry desert banks. The river occupies only a thin line along the channel of verdant growth.

Riparian Life

The springs are much more than the water released onto the ground surface. Take a cup of water out to a dry patch of dirt and carefully pour a small amount onto the surface. The margin between water and dry dirt can be compared to a riparian zone. The riparian zone is the line of transition between water and dry land where the soil is moist.

Riparian zones are found around any source of water, including rivers and lakes. Whether moving or static, if the water remains on the surface, grass and sedges will soon take root along the edges. In time the wind will carry the fluff of bulrushes to the stream or pond, possibly taking over every inch of open water.

The wind may also bring the downy seeds of the cottonwood to anchor and sprout in the moist earth. The cottonwoods are the marker for the presence of water in the desert even when no surface water is evident.

As vegetation increases around the spring, the invertebrates begins to move in. Some of these are so small they are nearly invisible to the naked eye, but like us, without water they will die.

The Santa Catalinas are a mountain range formed by rock pushed from deep under the surface to tower over the desert plain. In the foothills along the base of the range, small springs have appeared along the fault lines. I was discussing these springs with Samantha Hammer from the Sky Island Alliance one afternoon.

"We found springsnails in one of the springs," Sami exclaimed.

Great, snails! I thought of the slimy trails left by a creature, the bane of gardeners.

I learned that springsnails as an *endemic* species are important in understanding the health of a spring. Springsnails are invertebrates, meaning they have no backbone. The shell protects their soft tissues. They live within an aquatic environment, like the springs, feeding on algae. Generally, they will not survive in water that is polluted. When researchers find springsnails they get excited as they know the water that is emerging from the spring is uncontaminated.*

Hurray for springsnails!

The riparian zone of a small spring can be extremely fragile. In our arid land, we can appreciate how important the riparian zones are to each of us, whether we are speaking of small invertebrates living on algae in a spring or a teenager with an inner tube picking a path through thorny brush to splash into cool, river water. A spring supports life from the smallest invertebrate to larger creatures like elk, bears and mountain lions.

The riparian zone also slows erosion with the roots of vegetation helping to retain the soil. When the researchers from the Springs Institute and the Sky Island Institute begin to work with a spring, they first assess the condition of the spring and lay out a course of action. A grid is laid across the spring and surrounding riparian zone, using small stakes and string. They begin to catalogue the species of plants and animals found in each square of the grid as they want to know what depends on the spring for life.

Imagine sinking your feet into wet soil, thick with clay, that clings to every inch of your shoes, squishing down into your toes. The teams from these two institutes spend hours hunched over a grid, counting every growing thing within a square foot, from grass to invertebrates to small insects.

They examine the damage done to the spring. Sometimes this is due to storms that flood the natural watercourse or to wildlife that tear up the soft earth with sharp hooves, destroying the natural vegetation. Without sufficient vegetation, the water from the spring begins to carve a course that will allow the water from the spring to move faster, sweeping top soil downstream. In time the channel grows deeper, forming high banks. Sediment may shift, obscuring the natural outlet of the spring. As natural vegetation dies back, invasive species may become established.

The riparian zone can be made up of multiple microhabitats, meaning distinct species live in the conditions of a particular habitat. If removed from their habitat at a particular spring, they may not survive when transplanted to another

---

* The springsnails of Montezuma Well being the exception! Endemic means native to a community or ecosystem.

> **The Species Found in Fossil Creek**
> The water emerging in Fossil Springs has a high concentration of calcium carbonate and dissolved carbon dioxide. The later may account for the bubbles that appear with some of the springs that emerge within the stream. The water carries dissolved solids that are the building blocks of travertine found along the Fossil Creek and Pine Creek at Tonto Natural Bridge. This riparian zone has a a diverse number of species.
> * 166 distinct plant species thrive along the pools above the dam.
> * Native fish include the headwater chub, the roundtail chub, the speckled dace, the longfin dace, the desert sucker and the Sonoma sucker.
> * 147 species of macroinvertebrates including springsnails and the Page caddisfly.
> * 5 species of birds on the Federal Watch List including the bald eagle, the Mexican spotted owl, the Southwest flycatcher, the Yuma clapper rail and the yellow-billed cuckoo. All of these species remain important to the health of Fossil Creek.

spring since the conditions are diverse from their specific adaptation.

Dr. Larry Stevens notes that specific plants may be found with each type of spring. In higher elevations, it is common to find the maidenhair fern in a hanging garden. A hillslope spring might shout its presence through the bright yellow and red tones of rudbeckia. The rheocrene spring may announce its presence with clumps of willow along the streambed below the outlet. One of the most common species is the bullrush, a member of the sedge family, that seems to show up along the edges of any perennial pool of water. Poison ivy also makes an appearance around many of the springs.

In studies of the Colorado River Basin, researchers found a total of 79 endemic or native species present at many of the springs. Among the invertebrates, researchers look for springsnails, beetles and water bugs, amphipods, dragonflies and damselflies. Vertebrates include the smallest frogs, joined by mammals including the massive elk and illusive mountain lion.

Not all the species present are desirable. Crayfish have become a major threat at almost every stream and lake in the southwest. Crayfish, which resemble a miniature lobster, will quickly devour native species, including small snakes. Bullfrogs are also known to decimate native species. The mosquitofish, with the bass and bluegill, were introduced into the state's waterways. These species now compete with native fish.

The riparian zones are a whole eco-system within a small area. Some are just a few yards wide while others stretch for miles, depending on the size of the spring and the geography surrounding it. As part of our respect for the world around us, we stop at the edge of such a zone and become aware of where we are treading. Our feet, clad in modern footware, could wipe out a significant portion of some unique species. Rather than bumbling through the muck, we can sit and quietly observe the life around us.

Historically, we may have downplayed the importance of the role the springs play in our arid state. Starting with the Spanish entradas in the 1500's, men brought cattle and livestock into Arizona. Little was done to protect the springs from the hooves of livestock.

The Environmental Protection Agency began to lay out some regulations for our water resources in the late 1900s. One of the regulations required springs used for human consumption be protected from contamination. With many of the springs, this came to mean that a cement box was constructed around the outlet. Other springs were capped, the water directed into a reservoir. While the regulations intended well, they were not necessarily good for the riparian zones that existed around the springs. If the water was contained, then the riparian zone began to dry out. Small animals could not obtain water from cement spring boxes without the risk of falling in and drowning. Even large mammals could not access the largest metal tanks.

Both the Springs Institute and the Sky Island Institute were not satisfied with merely cataloging the springs but began to work at restoring a few of the springs. Some have been altered to the point where they cannot be restored. Others have simply disappeared due to redirection or dropping aquifers.

As we move forward, we need to recognize that springs are more than just a water faucet for the aquifers that silently move through the rocks under our feet. They are a calling card for the aquifers, inviting us to consider how the environment around us has been formed and how it functions.

In the pages that follow, I will introduce some of the springs that have been significant in the development of Arizona. Others are simply interesting for their formation or some unique feature that draws attention.

O'Neil Spring: After a wet winter, water pours out of the hillside in Kachina Village, down the slopes of Pumphouse Wash to flood the wetlands west of I-17. The geese and mallards gather in the ponds celebrating the arrival of spring. These wetlands are an important stop for migrating birds along the west coast flyways.

Bottom Photo: A water weir used to measure the number of gallons flowing from O'Neil spring.

Spitz Spring

Part II

Spring Narratives

Life Emerging

A hiker venturing through a narrow canyon stumbled across a pair of sticks bound with sinew, one blue, the other green. A closer look revealed a small bag of corn pollen attached to the sticks along with a feather or two. Many native Americans would recognize both the object and the location.

In this canyon, sheer vertical walls frame a narrow stream of water trickling along the canyon floor. After a good rain or above average snowmelt, the canyon can be a maelstrom of brown water pouring over rock ledges, surging against the rock walls.

On this warm spring day, the trickle came from a travertine mound seeping water into the Little Colorado. Stay away! Do not climb to the summit of the mound for this is sacred ground for the Hopi people. The Hopi call the spring *Sipapuni*, or *Sipapu*, the place of emergence. The sticks represent Hopi prayers presented to the spirits or katsinas who govern their world.

Springs have long been set apart as sacred among the native people. Montezuma Well is the site of emergence for the Yavapai. After a baby is born, traditional Navajo parents will visit the well to draw water to wash the hair of a newborn child.

Big Spring on the North Rim of the Grand Canyon is sacred to the Paiute people. I've been told women are not allowed to touch the water flowing from the spring. Only the men may advance to the edge of the stream, to dip their hands in the water. The Tohono O'odham consider the spring in Ventana Cave to be sacred in their history as it played a significant role in a great flood.

Not only is Sipapuni sacred, the Hopi are reluctant to allow visitors to come near any of their springs in the northern mesas where they make their homes. Their beliefs go beyond the geomorphology of the spring to another dimension. The believe that just as water sustains life, so a spring can be the place where life is born. A spring is to be held in reverence.

Scientific belief removes the sacred and looks at a spring from what can be touched, what can be seen and what is measured. We ask how the water emerges in this place? Where did the water come from? How long has it flowed? Time immemorial? How can we measure the flow of the spring? While we cannot see the moment when the Creator brought forth life, we can turn to the work of archeologists to gain a perspective on the springs, reaching back into ancient history. Several sites grant a glimpse into the springs before scientific records were kept.

The Verde Valley

We began with Montezuma Well, a limnocrene spring. Archeological digs suggests the Verde Valley may have been inhabited for at least 8,000 years before the Spanish arrived. Around 50 sites, each with at least 25 rooms, have been discovered at two-mile intervals along the river.

Montezuma Well may not have provided drinking water but Beaver Creek and the Verde River were certainly perennial sources of water. Verde Hot Springs, and further south, Castle Hot Springs, were important to the health of native people. Archeologist Matt Gebhard suggests that the Verde Valley became a major trading center between the northern tribes and those who lived in the south.

While the early tribes could rely on the Verde River for irrigation, and further south, on the Gila and the Salt, in some areas the larger springs would have been channeled to provide water to terraced gardens. Medicinal plants found in the riparian zone would have been highly valued.

Ventana Cave

In the 1940's, archeologist Emil Haury directed two teams excavating the floor of Ventana Cave. In an archeological dig, successive layers of dirt are removed from a series of trenches. The dirt was carefully sifted to reveal objects that may have lain buried for centuries. In the upper levels, the researchers found objects from the Tohono O'odham culture. In lower levels, researchers discovered objects, including stone points with wood tools and bone from what is believed to be the Hohokam culture along with several graves. The Tohono O'odham say they descended from the Hohokam.

Futher digging revealed more bones and stone projectiles that seem to date back as far as 11,000 BC, later revised to 8,800 BC. Think back 8,000 years to a time when man may have struggled out of the frozen waste of the Arctic, after crossing the Bering Strait. He moved south, most likely along the shore of the North American continent until the massive fields of ice receded and he discovered a land with green vegetation and abundant animals to provide food. Moving inland, he followed the rivers that seeped from the ice packs. The surveys at Ventana Cave indicate that one of the earliest cultures in North America may have chosen to settle in this region near water seeping from the rock.

They left their signature at Ventana Cave in the form of a small bone from an ancient creature that resembled our modern horse. That bone tells us that at one point a hunter crouched over a small seep of water trickling from the stone wall of the cave. Scooping water into his open mouth, he quenched his thirst.

The spring in Ventana Cave has given water for a very long time, back to a time when the earth was still settling into it current geography.

We stopped at the Hickiwan District office and met Chairman Manual Osequeda. His is not an office frequented by white tourists but rather an office for the business of the Tohono people. The landscape is swathed in tones of brown grit and desert grass rising to meet the vast sky. Dwarfed by this panaroma, a small school sits to one side of a dirt lot. A row of trucks and vans lined the front of the office building, adding a splash of color. The wind swept dust into a whirlwind, scouring the parking lot before passing into the field of sagebrush.

Five Tohono O'odham faces turned as we entered the building, each expressionless as one woman asked what business I might have in the Hickiwan district. Instead of launching into my list of questions, I stopped to admire several gleaming three-foot high trophies that lined one wall. We learned that the teenagers of the tribe play a game based on a sport once played by the Hohokam with a stick

The Tohono O'odham value two elements along with life itself: water, of course, and salt.

The Salt Trail

Without salt and the essential minerals, the body fades and loses its vitality.
For centuries the Tohono O'odham walked across the Gran Desierto, skirting El

Pinacate, an extinct volcano, to the Gulf of California. This is one of the driest places on earth. In the depressions along the shoreline of the Sea of Cortez, the incoming tide deposits minerals rich in salt. As the water evaporates, huge salt flats form.

As we drove through the Hickiwan District, we crossed the path of four men. Single file they strode along the road, looking neither left or right, but keeping a steady pace forward. Within a couple of miles we passed a fifth man leaning against the frame of his truck looking back along the road for a glimpse of the travelers.

In the district office, Chairman Manuel Osequeda held up a piece of salt.

"These men came by today to bring us a blessing, to show us favor. We would never ask for such a gift. It must be offered! This is very important to understand. Do not ask that someone bless you. It is for them to decide."

The Salt Trail, an ancient pilgrimage, traverses their traditional lands from Ajo down to Quitobaquito spring, just west of where traffic crosses the international border at Lukeville. Beyond the spring, the trail bisects what is known as Devil's

Entrance to Ventana Cave

Highway, or in Spanish, the Jornado del Diablo. In 1848, many gold miners pursuing the California Gold Rush perished along the Jornado.

The Tohono O'odham live 300 miles from the gulf but they are called the people of the sea by other O'Odham tribes. Their signature is the sea shell. They walk for ten days covering about thirty miles a day, exposed to the sun and the wind. Their feet pound hot gravel. Each carries a little water. In previous centuries there was no support vehicle where they might refill their canteens.

Upon reaching the salt flats on the Sea of Cortez, they collect the mineral and filter out the impurities. The salt forms a crusty rind with a bubbly appearance on one side. As they return, they stop to bless each community with salt. The people wait for their appearance. As we watched, their pace did not falter as they traded the lead, single file.

For the Tohono O'odham this is a sacred responsibility. Once a man sets his feet on the Salt trail, he must make the journey every year for the next ten years or risk a curse settling on him. Such a commitment is not taken lightly.

I've read accounts of those trapped by injury in the back country. They might have water from a stream or snowmelt but as the days pass, muscle cramps come from a lack of minerals. Such is the substance of life. The Tohono O'odham, the sand people of the Salt Trail, make their pilgrimage every year to restore the health of their people.

and a ball. The action is intense as each team strives to put the ball through the goal and the line of trophies indicate the teenagers from the Hickiwan district are adept at this game.

I next asked about the knowledge that has been passed down from previous generations on how the Tohono O'odham people have survived for so many centuries in such a forbidding environment. Much of the Tohono traditional knowledge in desert survival has been lost. Now the tribes depend on the gaming machines near Tucson and Ajo for their income. Chairman Osequeda is proud of the programs the tribe sponsors to help his people.

Ventana Cave Spring

The vice chairwoman assured me they still have a festival celebrating the blooming of the saguaro when wine and syrup are made from the blossoms and fruit born on the needle-studded cactus. We talk about the Salt Trail and the team of men who had just past through the office.

I turn my questions to Ventana Cave and Quitobaquito Spring. The Chairman indicates that all visitors must check in with his office before proceeding to the cave. The location is not well known and a young lady offers to show us the route.

We found the spring in a nearby range of hills. From the parking area, the cave's entrance appeared to be a large alcove at the base of a cliff. I expected a riparian zone to reveal the presence of the spring. No trace of water appeared. We dropped into a sandy wash before ascending a steep hill to the base of peak.

The Castle Mountains consist of ancient magma heaved skyward with intrusions from later volcanic activity. Surrounding the range are vast plains of sedimentary rock. The water in the spring is cold, with no hint of a volcanic eruption.

The region receives less than 10 inches of precipitation annually, leaving the soil bone dry. Cactus and mesquite accent the swirls of dust. The Tohono O'odham once called the cave *Chiu Vafia*, meaning spring cave. A second name has been given, *Hewultki,* meaning the house of the wind. Legend suggests that the wind prefers mesquite smoke. When workman built a fire from ironwood, the wind scattered the coals and the live embers caught the fibers of their blankets on fire.

In the 1930's Native Americans members with the Civilian Conservation Corps built a retaining wall across the rear of the cave to contain the water seeping from the rock. They bored into the rock wall, creating a tunnel and enlarged the pool. The water does not flow beyond the wall, effectively killing any riparian area that may have existed. The floor of the cave is dusty dry with an uneven surface left from previous excavations. The best of intentions have left the water inaccessible to any four-legged creature that might seek to quench its thirst. Bees cling to the moist wall above the water line.

Against the right-side of the cave is a square cement box, also dusty dry. At one time water was piped from the spring into the box for use by the Tohono O'odham.

One lone cottonwood marks the location of Quitobaquito pond.

Quitobaquito

Better known than Ventana Cave is Quitobaquito. Reaching back one thousand years, the spring was a primary source of water for the Tohono O'odham and the Hia-Ced O'odham as they trekked across the Sonoran desert. Quitobaquito served as a marker between the two branches of O'odham. Due to the extended use of the spring by both Spanish and American settlers in the 1800's, no archeological evidence remains of the earliest cultures.

Arriving at the spring, we first notice the heavy vegetation just north of the border, dominated by a 100 year-old cottonwood that stands sentry duty over a

Quitobaquito Pond

mesquite bosque (woodland). Following a foot-worn path through the brush, we found a large pond that seems out of character with the chalk-dry landscape. The edge of the pond is lined with scirpa sedge, a native reed that lends cover to the ducks that float across the surface of the water. The birds seemed unconcerned that we have arrived, choosing to dive head first to scavenge a meal in the growth along the bottom. Standing on the banks of the small pond, there is a quiet serenity that pervades the site.

When ancient native Americans first used the spring, a series of small depressions below the outlet contained the water. In 1863 Andrew Dorsey arrived at the spring and dug the first pond, building a berm to retain the water for livestock. Next, he dug irrigation ditches to water corn, melons and an orchard with fig and pomegranate trees. He added several small buildings, one of which was a small store. The store became something of a landmark for travelers between the small town of Nogales and the Sea of Cortez as Quitobaquito was the last source of water before crossing a hundred miles of desert. Dorsey went so far as to create small coins as tender for trade at his store. One of these coins was found during excavation at the spring.

In 1890 he sold his holdings to the Orosco family who lived on the site until they sold the property in July 1957 to the United States government as part of the plan to expand the monument. Jim Orosco, a descendent of the Hia C-ed was reluctant to sell the property. He had enlarged the pond to cover about a half acre to a depth of two feet. *

By 2005, the pond was losing a large amount of water and the Park Service was finding it difficult to maintain the water level. The Service enlarged and improved the depth of the basin in 2007. Much of the sedge and non-native species were removed.

As I walked around the pond I entered a small bosque of mesquite along a narrow channel with a trickle of water. The channel had been stabilized with a cement base. This ensures the water will reach the pond without disappearing into soil but it also prevents the water from saturating the roots of the mesquite. Then again, as a hillside spring, water may be flowing under the ground's surface. Today, natural mesquite bosques, a valuable resource, are disappearing in southern Arizona as the water table drops.

At the upper edge of the bosque I found a more natural channel, the trickle of water nearly hidden by deep grass. The spring emerges at the base of a large rock. The aquifer is recharged by rain filtering into the alluvial sediments and the cracks of the volcanic rocks in the Quitobaquito Hills just north of the spring. The aquifer flows in a southeastern direction along Aguajita Wash to emerge from both Quitobaquito Spring and nearby Aguajita Spring.

Quitobaquito Spring has two outlets emerging, one below the other, on the hillside. During the 2007 renovation, the lower outlet was channeled into a pipe that fed the pool while the upper outlet was allowed to flow along the surface. There are other two highly-mineralized seeps further west.

The spring is the home of several unique species including the scirpa sedge. The Sonoyta mud turtle burrows into the soft mud of the pond until just its nostrils

Quitobaquito spring & channel

*Today, Park management consults 16 different tribes, including the Hopi, before making significant changes at Quitobaquito.

are showing. Pupfish, an Arizona native, and the Quitobaquito springsnail are also present.

Records from the mid 1880s record this region as covered with grass growing as high as a horse's bridle. The grass was rooted in soil that had taken centuries to develop. When the Spanish, and later white settlers, brought cattle into the region, the grazing quickly stripped the soil of its cover. Strong monsoonal winds lifted the soil, leaving a scarred surface where the grass could not take root again. Cactus and desert plants flourished and dust became the hallmark of the desert plain.

This region receives on average nine inches of rain a year: arriving as summer monsoonal rains in July and August and winter storms in December and January. Desert sands with their granular structure can absorb large amounts of water. However, the desert soil has been baked and hardened by the sun. Water received from a microburst is more likely to run down into the washes with little being absorbed. Personnel at Lukeville, the border crossing near Quitobaquito, have recorded receiving two inches of rain in one hour from a microburst that sent water careening through desert washes.

Rijk Morawe, Park ranger, says that the aquifer under Quitobaquito at first has only a slight increase in output after a heavy storm with a stronger response two months after the rain has fallen. This suggests that the aquifer is fairly shallow. Based on carbon-dating tests, researchers believe the water has been held for 500 to a 1000 years. Organ Pipe NPS records shows that about every seven years, the area has above average rainfall which helps sustain the aquifer.

The Park Service has recorded about 11 springs throughout the Park, mostly located in the mountainous region. Another important source of water are the tinajas or rocky depressions that hold water left after a rainfall. While most evaporate fairly quickly a few retain water year-round for the population of Coues white-tail deer.

Crossing the border at Quitobabquite into Mexico in 2018 was not that difficult. A series of white posts and a vehicle barrier consisting of a low bar with upright steel posts marked the International border. On the Mexican side, large trucks and passenger cars raced past on a two-lane paved highway. Upon returning to the small parking lot, we found a Border Patrol truck with six large tires wired to lay horizontally between two posts. The Border Patrol officer was assigned to drag the tires along the verge of the dirt road for miles. Later patrols would check the drag strip for footprints, indicating that a group of men and women had crossed the border without first obtaining permission to enter the United States.

In late 2019, Quitobaquito is facing a new threat. Large groups of Central American refugees were brought to the border near Quitobaquito. They crossed the vehicle barrier and walked the few yards to the dirt road on the American side of the international border.

The plain beyond the spring is populated with cactus and thorny brush. In the summer months, temperatures soar well above 100 degrees, leaving the area inhospitable to those on foot. Quitobabquito is the last remaining source of perennial water for miles to come.

When agents from the Border Patrol arrive, the refugees asked for asylum and to be taken to the processing center to begin the process of establishing their claim. For months the border had been in an uproar over the large caravans that have traveled north from El Salvador and Honduras, their participants seeking relief from unemployment and the violence of gangs that terrorized many of the poor neighborhoods.

As a nation, attempting to live according to our laws, immigrants are expected to apply for a permit to legally immigrate into the United States. Unfortunately, the demand exceeds the quotas set by the United States in keeping with providing our native born citizens with employment and housing opportunities. A whole industry has developed over the last century and a half to smuggle people, beginning with the Chinese laborers, into the United States. The Central American refugees are the latest to seek a new life in a land that stands as a beacon throughout the world for the opportunity to make a prosperous life.

In response to the flood of immigrants at our border, in 2019 the Trump administration began building a wall of steel along the dryland portions of the border. This was a double threat to the springs and the species that rely on them.

Once the wall is completed, larger species south of the border will now develop separately from the population to the north, reducing the genetic diversity in both populations. The O'odham have complained that this will also limit their access between tribal lands north and south of the border.

The second concern is the amount of water required to construct the wall. The footing for the wall will be concrete. Each cubic yard of concrete will require around 32 gallons of water. A linear foot of wall will require two cubic yards of cement. A mile is 5,280 linear feet, requiring 337,920 gallons of water. Where does this water come from in the middle of a desert?

The construction firm building the wall has proposed drilling wells to pro-

vide ground water to mix the concrete on site as well as dust control. The aquifer for the Quitobaquito spring is shallow. We can be fairly certain that such a major withdrawal would severely impact the flow from the spring. The United States Park Service, the agency responsible for protecting the spring, has requested wells be drilled no closer than five miles to Quitobaquito. The placement of these wells could be critical if they sink into the Aquajita Wash.

    Biologists are scrambling to remove the endangered species as well as unprotected species such as the tryonia snail, a mollusk smaller than a sesame seed, to a refuge where it is hoped they will survive and multiply. If the spring were to run dry, it is uncertain whether the rock fractures that support the spring would close, collapsing the aquifer. The Park Service as well as other interested parties will be closely watching the progress of the border wall and how the spring responds.

Manantiel de Agua

In 1540, a major expedition entered the territory that would come to be called Arizona. Set against a wide plain, under a brilliant blue sky, the entrada may have seemed insignificant. At the head of a long column led by Francisco Vasquez de Coronado rode men with steel helmets. They were followed by a thousand men on foot, carrying lances and bows. Then came supply wagons, creaking over the rough ground followed by herds of livestock snatching bits of brush as they were pushed onward by vaqueros.

The Tohono O'odham and other tribes further north would not have recognized how this entrada of men speaking a foreign tongue would be the vanguard of upheaval to all they had known. Consider the number of animals that would have been required to pull the supply wagons as well as the horses of the conquistadors. Each horse would require around 10 gallons of water every 24 hours. Add this to the water required by the men. From the records the Spanish kept, we learn that there was more ground water available in the southwest in the 16th and 17th centuries. The region was not the desert that it is today but temperatures remained high during the summer months when Coronado's expedition traveled north.

They most likely followed the Rio Sonora north to what is now Cananea, Mexico. Within a day's ride, the expedition would have reached the San Pedro River, a significant source of water. Most historians believe that Coronado led his men north up the Sulphur Springs Valley, a few miles east of the San Pedro River. Diaries from the expedition record that the men suffered terribly from the heat and deprivation as they struggled north into what was then called the Wilderness.

I've wondered about the springs along this route. Considering that the expedition would have required 2,500 to 3,000 gallons every 24 hours, where are the major springs that would have provided enough water for the animals and men?

The Sulfur Springs valley lies along a north-south axis. On the eastern edge are the Chiricahua Mountains that rise 6,000 feet above the valley floor. The Huachuca Mountains and the Dragoons line the western edge of the valley. Driving south from Interstate 10, the Wilcox Playa, a dry lake bed, spreads across the floor of the valley. Beyond the Playa, vast green fields lie on either side of the highway. The little farming town of Elfrida is the valley's heart. Where does the water come from to support these farms? There are no wide, slow-flowing rivers creasing the valley floor. The green fields of the Sulphur Springs Valley speak of the aquifer that lies below what was once arid land. The same arid land once crossed by Coronado's expedition.

Today, most of the springs in the valley are small. Some run dry during the warm months. Delbert Mortenson lived near the farming community of Elfrida in the 1920's, nearly 400 years after Coronado's expedition would have passed along this route. His memory of living in Elfrida helps us understand how the aquifer has changed and why the springs have either disappeared or decreased their flow.

"I can remember when I was a small child we would go out to Elfrida. They all had dug wells at that time. You could look down and the water was only 16 feet from the surface. Later, a fellow who was farming out there told me several years ago he was pumping from 265 feet. So they have depleted the water table . . . with all those farms in there. Of course there were no farms in there when they went homesteading there. The water flowed all the way down from Rucker Canyon clear into Whitewater (Elfrida). That is what they figured helped build the water table."

If water was flowing from mountain springs down into the valley we might understand why Coronado's scouts led him up the Sulfer Springs Valley. Nearly two fifths of the surface water in the Valley once drained into White Water Wash which nourished the aquifer. Now the aquifers have receded as the water table is drawn down by the agricultural industry that has fed our modern civilization.

Gi Vavhia

During the Spanish colonial period, Spanish friars moved north into the lands of the Pima and Tohono O'odham. As settlers followed, developing ranches and communities, the Viceroyalty sent soldiers to establish Presidios along the frontier. The first mission established in what would become Arizona was at Guevavi or *gi vavhia*, meaning 'big water' in the local dialect. Spanish records describe a spring flowing from a hillside above the Santa Cruz River. We visited the mission ruins near Tubac in February 2018. As we walked toward the site I gazed around, trying to imagine the area as it would have appeared in 1691. On this day, a light layer of clouds muted the sunlight. The wind, no pleasant breeze, whipped our hair, tearing at our clothes. It seemed in alliance with the desolate land surrounding us. Everywhere was gritty, desert sand.

The Patagonia Mountains loomed to the northeast. The mesquite and thorn brush looked winter dead, waiting for spring when a hint of green would steal along their limbs to erupt in minuscule leaves. Sidestepping the barren ant warrens, we moved along a narrow dirt track, seemingly oppressed by the grimness of a landscape wrung dry. There was not a spring in sight, nor a trickle of water. Not one drop of moisture clung to a tiny particle of sand or slender twig. The Park Service Ranger stopped abruptly and turned to face us.

"Ladies and gentlemen, welcome to the City of Nogales." No one said anything. I stared at the sand below his feet, aware of the direction of his conversation.

"You are currently standing over the aquifer for the City of Nogales. City wells are pumping this area dry." He pointed toward the dry watercourse nearby. "At one time the Santa Cruz river flowed past this site. Now, we only see water after a heavy monsoon storm."

The ruins of Guevavi Mission

Was there any evidence of a spring at the mission ruins? His answer lay in the dry, dusty ground with only the wind for company. This had been the complaint centuries earlier of a Jesuit priest assigned to this parish he would call the Mission of Sorrows. In a diary he bemoaned the wind as his constant and only companion.

The Sobaipuri, the Pima and at times the Tohono O'odham lived along the Santa Cruz. This stream flows north and provided a route for explorers intent on entering the southwest. Father Kino and Father Salvatierra arrived to find a number of native villages along the river. The Pima built brush shelters and planted small gardens that relied on irrigation. Priests following in their steps of Father Kino directed the tribal people to build the walls of the adobe mission. In the 18th century the three missions built along the Santa Cruz, provided a sense of safety and community for Spanish settlers.

In 1807, the Governor overseeing Tumacacori Mission applied for a land grant. This was followed by a second land grant in 1811 to Don Agustin Ortiz, protecting the legal status of the mission at Guevavi as well as the spring. The mission drew travelers as a reliable stop where they might restock their supplies.

Eighty years after the mission was founded, Juan Bautista de Anza, a Spanish Captain, would lead a band of settlers along this route as they traveled north to Monterey. The colonies along the eastern seaboard were just celebrating their Declaration of Independence from England.

One hundred and fifty years after de Anza's expedition, men driven to gamble their lives on rumors of gold along creeks in California would pass this way seeking their fortune. The missions at Guevavi, Tumacacori and Tucson with the spring at Quitobaquito drew travelers to this southern route.

As we stood on a shelf above the Santa Cruz, we looked down on dry, riven sand studded by small boulders between vertical banks. All that remains of Guevavi Mission are two adobe walls melting into the sands on the plain above the riverbed. Gi vavhia has disappeared. Curiously, a green pine stands not far from the mission. There may indeed be water beneath the surface.

As we returned along the road that led us to Guevavi, we passed a spring box built of mortar and stone near a small ranch. The ranch had a well with a windmill pulling water to the surface from the aquifer. As the windmill and the pumps for the City of Nogales bring water to the surface, the level of the aquifer is dropping.

The Presidio of Tucson

The Spanish moved beyond Guevavi, to establish a mission at Tumacacori. Father Kino then learned of a small Tohono O'odham village called Cuk Son near the headwaters of the Santa Cruz. He established another mission at what would become San Xavier del Bac.

Spanish settlers soon followed the priests, settling along the Santa Cruz. The Apaches did not fail to notice the new settlers with their modern firearms, horses and cattle. The livestock made the settlers a target for Apache raids. The settlers in turn petitioned the Viceroy in Mexico City for protection. In August 1775, a company of soldiers arrived to establish a Presidio on a shelf of land overlooking the Santa Cruz River. The water available from the river and from springs near the base of the Santa Catalinas played an important role in the founding of the Presidio near Cuk Son - or as we know it, the city of Tucson.

When the settlers first arrived they looked for a perennial source of water. At that time the Santa Cruz was a perennial stream. A forest of tall mesquite flourished along the banks of the river as a beautiful refuge for the settlers after their journey north. In the late 1800's the aquifer remained close to the surface and the springs continued to release water into the river's current. Today the Santa Cruz is a cement-lined ditch with a bed of dry sand and boulders running along the western side of the city. Bridges span the riverbed every mile or so.

Like many, I considered the Santa Cruz to be a river but Julia Fonseca, the

The Santa Cruz riverbed in Tucson was once lined with a mesquite bosque.

Pima County Office for Sustainability, offered another perspective. She first led me to a map of the corridor along the Santa Cruz that dated back to the early 1800s. There was the river as a line snaking across the map. Spreading out from either side were rectangular plots with Spanish names. Each plot, roughly outlined, represented the land owned by one of the families that lived near the Presidio. They would have planted corn, beans and squash. Irrigation ditches with rough wooden gates distributed water through irrigation canals to each plot of land. The Hohokam, who had lived in this region 500 years earlier, had used the same concept to bring water to their gardens.

    I stood looking at the map and thinking about how each family must have come to the region. The earliest arrivals would have claimed the land closest to the river while later arrivals would have settled on plots farther from the river. The late arrivals must have cast covetous glances at the well-established fields as they worked to dig ditches that would bring life-giving water to their fields. First the Spanish, then Mexico, held the Presidio despite periodic warfare with the Apaches until 1821. Anthropologists estimate the Spanish population did not rise over 500 people during that era.

    In 1890 and twice in the early 1900's, large floods swept down the river, destroying the fields and irrigation canals that had been so carefully tended for over a century. In the 1930's, turbine engine began to pull large quantities of water out of the aquifer. Much of the marshland along the river was drained for development, not incidently preventing plagues of mosquitos from tormenting residents. As the water table began to drop, the deep roots of the mesquite died and the bosque which had once provided a lovely green belt along the stream, disappeared. The floods opened the valley to rapid urban development. Housing developments began to rise from the ancient fields. By the late 1900's the banks of the river had been overlaid with cement, preventing any further riparian zone or the recovery of a mesquite forest that had once provided a green belt through the town.

As we settled down to talk about water in Pima County, Julia spoke of the Santa Cruz as a spring. The US Geological Survey in their reports revealed that the only water released from the aquifer at the Santa Cruz River was taking place upstream, near Rillito, well north of the Presidio location.* The aquifer is recharged by the water that sluices off the Santa Catalinas into the alluvial plain. From the aquifer the water follows a series of faults from the aquifer to the river bed.

I'm still thinking about the idea that the river could be considered a spring. I've seen streams sink into the sand, only to emerge downstream. Could this be a spring? Regardless of how you define it, the river was the lifeline, first for the Hohokam, then the Pimas and Tohono O'odham, followed by the Spanish.

Even as the river began to disappear, a second source of water lay farther east of the Santa Cruz near the foothills of the Santa Catalinas. Cienegas! The cienega traditionally means marshland. Large pools of stagnant water lay along the Tanque Verde Wash at the base of the Santa Catalina mountains. Those who lived closer to the mountains, away from the river, used these pools as a source of water. Algae and other water-based plants often covered the surface of the pools. The Spanish spoke of *aire malo* near the cienegas for the gas from rotting vegetation that floated on the surface of the water. Yet, for those living in an arid climate, water was too valuable to dismiss as *mal*.**

The Spanish named these pools of water La Cebadilla Cienega. I've tried to find a definition for Cebadilla and the closest I've come would be a reference to barley. The Spanish grew barley in the fields irrigated by the canals that spread out from the Santa Cruz River. In the historical account of General Crook's time in Arizona, his biographer describes seeing the fields of barley as the troops approached the town of Tucson in the late 1800's.

La Cebadilla is located along the Santa Catalina detachment. As part of the Madrean archipelgo, much of the Catalinas is metamorphic rock pushed upward by pressure deep within the earth. Over the centuries water has carved deep

---

* In Part III, we discuss how water has begun to flow along the Santa Cruz River across the San Xavier Reservation once again.

** The illness described by the Spanish and early white settlers may have begun with the pits beneath outhouses that were dug alongside some of the wells near the Presidio. The sewage may have seeped into the shallow water table polluting the drinking water. The barley fields and refuge pits are described in On the Border with Crook by John G. Bourke.

La Cebadilla Cienega

I moved toward a patch of green grass and suddenly pulled back in complete shock. The green surface was not grass but algae floating on the surface of a lagoon. The pond's surface was completely hidden by patches of green and brown aquatic vegetation. I had been about to step off the embankment into a pool of water. There was no guessing the depth and I had no desire to step into the pond. Around me small frogs exploded into action, leaping from the leaf litter to the safety of the pond. Plop, plop! I jumped with each small cannonball.

    I gazed in complete wonder at the pool, feeling as if I had stepped through some sort of portal into a bayou. This was a natural 'cienega' more accurately identified as a limnocrene spring. The water was leaking through the earth's surface to form the pond. Now I understood how the early settlers could have valued the cienega as a primary water source. The Spanish rewarded this cienega with a unique name, La Cebadilla.

canyons through the granite and gneiss formations, sweeping the alluvial fill into the basin below. The layers of alluvium now serve as reservoirs. The aquifer under the Santa Cruz River valley has long supported human civilization but is now nourished by a second source of water we will discuss in Part III. La Cebadilla still exists on private property along the Tanque Verde Wash.

The San Jose de Sonoita Land Grant

In the early 1700s much of the land in what is now southeastern Arizona was covered with grass, watered by small streams. The Spanish, and later the American settlers, saw the potential in the grasslands for raising cattle. When the mining industry discovered gold near Nogales, and later silver in the Mule Mountains, the cattlemen in southern Arizona found a market for their cattle.

Sonoita Creek is located east of Tubac and Tumacacori. At one time, the perennial watercourse flowed into the Santa Cruz River near Nogales. As Spanish vaqueros moved into this region, they introduced cattle to the Sonoita Creek and San Pedro River watersheds. Under Spanish Colonial law, the Spanish settlers could request *sitios* or grants of land for grazing from the Spanish governor.

In early 1821, Leon Herreros, a resident at the Tubac Presidio, rode east toward an abandoned Indian village called Sonoita. The land was lush with grass. The perennial stream would satisfy the thirst of his cattle. That May, he applied to Antonio Cordero, the Governor of Sonora, for two sitios along Sonora Creek. One sitio equaled about 4,338 acres. The site was located eight leagues (20 miles) from Tubac. Even as he wrote out his petition for the sitio, Herreros acknowledged that this region was plaqued by attacks from the Apache raiding parties. He must have thought the cattle he hoped to raise were worth the risk.

The property was appraised at 60 pesos per sitio because it contained surface water. When sold at auction, Herreros paid 105 pesos, including the fees for the transaction. He was now in possession of some of the finest grazing land in this region. After purchasing the land, he obtained cattle from the mission at Guevavi and drove his herd east to the grasslands at the foot of the Patagonia Mountains. The land grant was called San Jose de Sonoita.

Sonoita Creek is fed by a series of springs that rise from an aquifer formed by the Santa Rita Mountains to the west and the Huachuca Mountains on the east. The creek descends along the southern edge of the Santa Rita Mountains flowing toward Nogales and would have been a beautiful home for the ambitious Herreros. The flaw in his plan was the raiding parties of the Apache Indians.

First Spain, then Mexico settled for a policy of appeasement with the Apaches. When the Mexican government became strapped for cash, the payments ended. The Apaches returned to raiding ranches and homesteads along the border. As white settlers began to move into the southwest, homesteads and ranches, including all of the land grants along the border had been abandoned.

Sonoita Creek watershed

The native villages that once harbored families of Pima and Tohono O'odham stood empty as the population moved north, closer to the protection of the Presidio in Tucson.

The white settlers, many from Texas, came to establish homesteads along the US-Mexico border. They had little regard for the claims of ownership by Mexican citizens. This led to years of legal action to settle ownership of valuable grazing land along the streams.

Let's take a look at two areas, including land that was once part of the San Jose de Sonoita land grant. Both Cienega and Sonoita Creeks rise out of this basin, receiving water from the Santa Rita Mountains to the west and the Whetstones and the Huachucas to the east.

Cienega Creek rises in the foothills of the Santa Rita Mountains to flow east through the grasslands before turning north toward Tucson. As with so many perennial water courses in the southwest, the banks of Cienega Creek have revealed evidence of early people groups living in this watershed. Pottery shards, tools and and small bones have been found in prehistoric sites.

About fifteen miles north of Sonoita, a dirt road turns east off State Route 82, taking visitors to the headquarters of the old Empire Ranch established in the 1860's. The original homestead was located on 160 acres with a four-room adobe ranch house. Over the next 20 years, ranch holdings grew to over 100,000 acres, which included some important springs. In 1988, through a series of land exchanges, the Bureau of Land Management acquired the ranch holdings. The

Cienega

Bureau established Las Cienegas National Conservation Area as a means of preserving this historic and unique region from development and mining interests.

Much of the rain and snow that fall on the Santa Rita and Whetstone Mountains drains into an aquifer that underlies the basin. The name Las Cienegas gives us a clue as to the nature of the springs on the ranch. Driving northeast from the ranch house, the road crosses Cienega Creek. In the shallow arroyo we found water trickling through a quagmire obscured by the clump grass shaded by tall cottonwood trees. The ground's surface appeared to be torn by the hoofs of livestock stopping to quench their thirst in the water that has pooled in small depressions.

Further downstream, we found a large pool nearly obscured by water-borne growth for wildlife and domestic stock. A woodland of well-spaced velvet mesquite, Goodding willow, Arizona ash, hackberry and Fremont cottonwood filled the large channel - a refuge to the animals and birds that live on the plain. Across southern Arizona cienegas such as this one have long been recognized as a valuable resource. The upper basin Cienega Creek, as part of the State Preserve, supports threatened and endangers species of native fish.

When mule trains first came through this area enroute to the mines further south, the drovers were careful to avoid the lower parts of the basin. They describe the central region as a bog which would be very different from the land today. Imagine how close to the surface the water table must have been in the late

Cienega Creek pond

1800s. The water table has been receding for the last 75 years.

Cienega Creek flows north from the grasslands of the Empire Ranch toward Tucson, entering Pantano Wash as it descends from the Whetstone Mountains. This large wash, one of the major watercourses that crosses Tucson, is dry throughout the year except when the monsoons hurl their torrents of rain against the dry land. The desert, unable to absorb the amount of water that descends in just minutes, sends the brown swirling current downstream to the Santa Cruz. This points to a less understood value of the grasslands. In maintaining the ground cover, the desert soil is able to retain more water than the scarified desert, allowing it to filter down to the aquifers. Without the grass cover, the water would disappear quickly downstream.

The grasslands are a transition zone between the Sonoran and Chihuahuan deserts, serving as an undeveloped corridor for the wildlife that travel through the region. Geologists estimate that the basin between the ranges may have been up to 5,000 feet deeper than what we now witness, with the top 100 feet being alluvial fill from the streams that descend from the surrounding ranges. In the upper basin, the aquifer flows toward the northeast, away from Sonoita while in the lower basin, the flow follows Pantano Wash toward the northwest.

Sonoita Creek also rises out of the south end of the basin between the Santa Ritas Mountains and the Canelo Hills. A geographic divide sends the stream south toward Nogales in a corridor between the Patagonia Mountains and the Santa Ritas. Several small springs, including Monkey and Alamo springs, lie along this route and mark the aquifer's southwest flow toward the Santa Cruz

River Valley.

While the upper region is dry most of the year, water remains in the creekbed as it passes through Sonoita and Patagonia to a wildlife preserve, helped in part by the Patagonia Waste Treatment Plant. Beyond the preserve the stream enters Patagonia Lake and Patagonia State Park. The last stretch of streambed is within Sonoita Creek State Natural Area, managed by Arizona State Parks. The stream enters the Santa Cruz River at Rio Rico, between the historic sites of Guevavi and Tumacacori Missions. This is the land that lured Leon Herrero to risk the threat of Apache raiding parties.

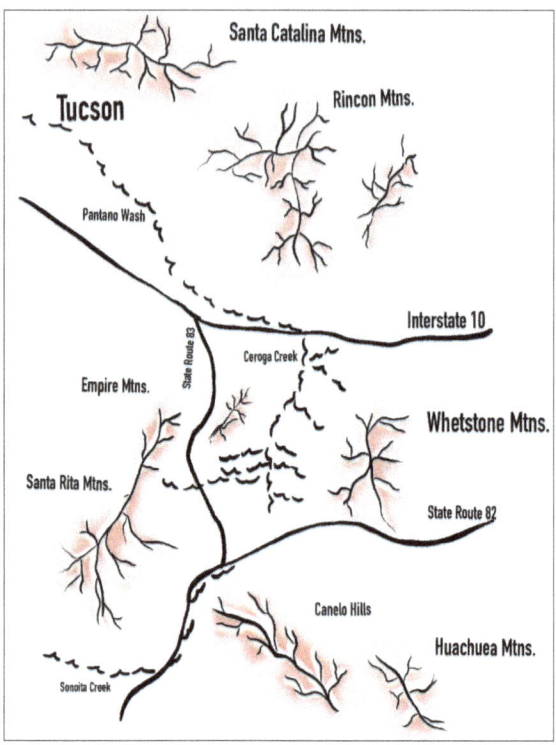

I am certain that the woman turning a faucet handle in the village of Patagonia gives little thought to the origin of Sonoita Creek. The water in her sink appears so easily with just a twist of a handle. It is unlikely that Sonoita Creek would still exist without the devoted efforts of conservationists, Arizona State Parks and the Bureau of Land Management to preserve Las Cienegas and the stream corridor from further development.

We began looking for Monkey Spring as part of the headwaters of Sonoita Creek. The name seems out of place as there are no wild monkeys in the southwest. Early settlers who first approached the spring came across a large family of wild coatimundis. These animals are native to southern Arizona but not well-known by modern city dwellers. I've long enjoyed watching their antics as they scurry along, tails erect, poking their long noses into crevices and under logs. They have long claws that allow them to quickly dig into insect nests and overturn small logs that might hide the next meal.

We found we could not approach Monkey Spring. Each road seemed to have a locked gate forbidding trespassers on the property. The Rail X Ranch is owned by Vaughan Galen who does not tolerate uninvited guests rolling across his sun-struck acres. We settled for visiting Alamo, a second spring rising in the foothills of the Sonoita Creek watershed. It had been a dry year and we were to find that the spring was nothing more than a damp rock face nearly obscured by brush.

Swimming at Monkey Springs: Nicholas Randolph, Margie Vail, Tom Vail, Bill Vail, 1923. The Vail family developed the Empire Ranch along with their holdings on the coast of California. Used by permission of the Empire Ranch Foundation

A footpath led us through thorny brush and shin stickers into a shallow canyon till we found a patch of damp ground. Working uphill from the damp soil, we reached a large rock projecting from the hillside. A few beads of water coursed along the face of the rock. The water had worked its way to the surface along a fault, revealing the presence of the aquifer. The fault is revealed on the surface by a shallow canyon. Incidently, there are at least four other Alamo springs in Arizona - it's a popular name.

There are tiny springs like this throughout southern Arizona. Many have disappeared with the years of drought. Others have been reduced to a patch of damp earth, a few drops sliding across a stone face. Once these springs were the lifeblood of the grasslands that drew the

Alamo Spring

cattlemen to southern Arizona. Cattle were allowed to overgraze the range, damaging the ecosystem. Today, the damage comes from the population boom. Once isolated ranches dotted this region. Today, the road above Alamo spring is lined with homes, each on a parcel of land. Many of these homes depend on wells that draw water from the aquifer that feeds Alamo spring. Across this region, the water is being removed from the aquifer faster than it can be replaced. This is justified by saying, "We need water to live."

That statement fails to recognize that we should have questioned the rate of growth long before the developers first began speculating over the vast acreage. When the aquifer fails, we will shrug and say, "This is a desert. What did you expect?" thus minimizing our role in overdrawing this resource.

The Patagonia-Sonoita Creek Preserve

The watershed for Sonoita Creek, spreads over 100 square miles, rising between the Santa Rita Mountains and the Canelo Hills to flow south, then west toward the Santa Cruz River at Rio Rico. Historically, the plain along Sonoita Creek was a marshland as the water exceeded the channel to create a much larger riparian zone than is now present. Hydrogeologists suggest that the alluvial deposits in the streambed could be up to 90 feet deep, providing water to the rheocrene springs in the channel. After a heavy monsoonal rain, the creek can still flood and remind residents that this is a flood zone.

Below Patagonia, the Nature Conservancy supports a 350-acre wildlife refuge. Hiking trails cross an open field to enter a woodland with some of the oldest Fremont cottonwood and Goodding willow in the state. Over 300 species of birds either make their home at the refuge or pass through on seasonal migration.

As I interviewed the Refuge Director, I noticed a bright red patch clinging to a sapling near the building. The Director identified the bird as a Scarlet Tanager, a bird more often found in the eastern woodlands. I'm not sure how such a bird would escape the sharp-eyed gaze of a raptor. The bright red color stood out like a sore thumb in the muted tones of green and brown across the refuge.

I hiked along the Preserve's trails, stepping off a berm to the creek to marvel at the bright green watercress and duckweed along the banks. In places this water loving species hid any glimpse of the flowing water beneath its green leaves. Early settlers used the watercress as part of their diet.

> **A Birder's List on Sonoita Creek**
> green kingfisher
> thick-billed kingbird,
> gray hawk
> vermilion flycatcher
> scarlet tanager
> violet-crowned hummingbird
> black-bellied whistling duck
> rose-throated becard
> northern beardless-tyrannulets
> zone-tailed hawk
> white-throated sparrows
> Over 20 species of flycatchers have been recorded on the preserve, as well as 130 species of butterflies.

Recycled effluent from Patagonia supplements the creek flowing through the Patagonia-Sonoita Creek Preserve. Mature cottonwood are struggling with the drought.

I gazed upward at 130 year-old cottonwoods, some of the trunks easily two to three feet in diameter. Elsewhere along the creek, I found huge cottonwoods lying on the ground, unable to sustain their weight since the region's drought had diminished the stream flow. In recent years this region has seen 40 percent less rainfall than in the 1990s. Flooding along the sandy streambanks once helps the cottonwood germinate. With low flows, the stream has cut into the banks, reducing the habitat for young willow trees to replace the fallen giants.

Examining the trees, I am reminded that there is subterranean water present. While little water may be visible in the upper watershed, water flows along the lower stretch of streambed into the reservoir at Patagonia State Park. Where did the water come from? Along the route, small rheocrene springs have contributed to the stream's flow. Treated effluent also swells the flow. Both stream and subsurface flow sustain the huge cottonwoods and a vital riparian refuge along Sonoita Creek.

The Refuge is a place where urban dwellers can come into finger-tip contact with a riparian zone. Visitors come from around the world to sit and observe over 300 species of birds in the Preserve. Mammals, large and small, step from the shadows of the woodland to sip the clear water. Both coatimundi and whitetail deer are common in the Refuge.

In the past, I followed the shallow stream under the tall cottonwoods near Patagonia Lake. Not another person shared this quiet corner of the refuge as I strolled along the water's edge, drawn onward by the bird calls and trickle of running water.

San Bernardino National Wildlife Refuge

The San Bernardino National Wildlife Refuge and the historic Slaughter Ranch are one of the best kept secrets in Arizona. My husband recalls his father driving from Bisbee to Slaughter's Ranch to fish. His dad was not satisfied to dip a line in the pond on the American side of the border. He would jump the fence and head for the pools on the Mexican side. No one seemed to be disturbed by this practice. After hearing their stories, Slaughter's Ranch was calling me.

We drove east out of Douglas, the paved road turning to dirt. The dust boiled from under our vehicle leaving an airborne trail, tracking our progress. Each desert shrub and cactus along the road seemed to be coated with layers of chalky dust. The green of the rolling hills around Douglas gave way to the Chihuahua desert. Somewhere up ahead I believed there was water flowing along the ground's surface. Nothing along the route would have led me to believe that there was a vast aquifer under our tires.

We passed through the main gate and crossed a small rise. The horizon bloomed in a brilliant green as if we had moved from a black and white monochrome to living color. Without doubt we had reached water!

Before the arrival of the Spanish, the Opata tribe planted small fields near the springs, channeling water to their crops. In the 1700's, the Apaches migrated into the region and were drawn to the springs as well. The springs would have seemed a refuge from the rocky redoubts of the Chiricahua and Swiss Elm Mountains to the north.

During their initial period of settlement, the Spanish built a Presidio about a mile south of the current international border. The site is visible across the border from Slaughter's Ranch. The San Bernardino Presidio was one of three across the northern border of New Spain. After Mexico gained its independence, Em-

peror Augustin Iturbidi granted 73,240 acres around the springs to Lieutenant Ignacio Perez for the sum of 90 pesos. Perez built a large ranch house at the site of the abandoned Presidio. He brought horses, mules and cattle to graze the rich grasslands. The future should have been bright.

To the Apaches, the ranch must have seemed to be a livestock market. By 1830, only eight years after purchasing the land grant, the Perez family abandoned the ranch, forced out by the violence of the Apache raids. For almost two decades the adobe buildings were the home of rodents and raptors with the walls melting into the sands.

The Mexican-American War ended in 1848 and a few months later word spread along the eastern seaboard of a gold strike in California. Men and women made their way west, either overland or by sea, to the gold fields. One route was along the Southern Emigrant Trail with the Butterfield stagecoach. The trail left Santa Fe, New Mexico, dropping south along the Rio Grande Valley, before turning west toward the southwestern corner of New Mexico and the springs on the international border. William Hunter, a 'Forty-niner', describes finding buildings with walls still standing around a square. He speculates that the ranch must have once been inhabited by up to 400 people.

The Mormon Battalion marched along this route in 1846, during the Mexican-American War. The route was most likely selected due to the availability of water.

Of the springs he writes, *"We here found an excellent spring a few yards to the left of the road ... This stream does not deserve the name of "River", with which Mexican bombast has invested it, as it is invisible, except where a few holes too deep for rushes to thrive in present their surfaces to the sky. A fine and extensive vale extends E, N and South from the Rancho, covered with coarse grass in most places taller than a man. Some little distance to the west commences a bench of level land covered with Cedar, Mezquite and Shrubs."*

Many of the emigrants camped at the springs, allowing their livestock a day or two of rest as they filled water barrels and washed clothing. From the springs, the trail turned west below the international border. The stagecoaches followed the Santa Cruz north, past Guevavi, Tumacacori and San Xavier del Bac missions enroute to Tucson and the Gila River.

Always looking for a faster route, the emigrants soon established the Tucson cut-off, completely bypassing the springs. The cut-off led gold miners through a pass on the north end of the Chiricahua Mountains with a stagecoach station at Apache Spring and a second stop on the north end of the Dragoons at Dragoon spring. From Tucson, the miners could travel north to intersect the Gila, following the river to the Colorado and the crossing at Yuma. This route was also known as the Gila or Kearny trail.

Many would-be miners impatient with the longer route turning north to the Gila, chose to risk traveling the Camino del Diablo or Devil's highway along what is now the international border. From Guevavi Mission, the men would travel west to Quitobaquito spring. Beyond Quitobaquito, the miners faced 100 miles of bone-dry Sonoran desert before reaching rain-filled pools in the Tinajas Altas Mountains. Coming from the east coast, they could not begin to fathom how the dry heat sucked every drop of moisture from their bodies. Some died just yards away from the water that would have saved them.

This was a desert the Tonono O'odham knew well. They knew the pockets of water called *tinajas* and the two seasons that filled the tinajas. Today, this route is Highway 2 in the desert state of Sonora.

The treaty ending the Mexican-American War gave the United State vast tracts of land across the southwest. In 1854, the United States purchased additional territory from Mexico under the Gadsden Purchase and initiated a survey of the border. As part of the Boundary Commission, men from both Mexico and the United States worked in unison to survey the border. Their official report describes the area around the San Bernardino ranch.

"Adjoining the ranch are numerous springs, spreading out into rushy ponds *and giving issue to a small stream of running water. The valley is covered with a coarse growth of grass."*

American settlers could now legally establish homesteads in the southwest. During the late 1870's and early 1880's, men came to reside in the borderlands of southern Arizona. Many of these men worked on the local ranches and were not concerned about living by the dictates of the Territory's Legal Code. They came to be known as the 'Cowboys.'

When the Cowboys, including the Clanton family, brought their personal code of ethics to Tombstone, the residents looked to the Earp brothers to counter the threat of the Cowboys. After the infamous gunfight, the Earps found it best to depart for California as their lives were now forfeit to men less concerned with the law than settling a score. The Cowboys, however, did not move on and the region continued to struggle with their misdeeds. The residents of Bisbee and Tombstone looked for an honest man to run for sheriff. Texas John Slaughter was that man and he had come to Arizona to raise cattle.

John Slaughter understood the threat that the Apaches brought to settlers along the border when he bought the ranch sight unseen in 1884. Before he could settle on his new property, the residents of Bisbee asked Slaughter to run for sheriff. John stood just over five feet tall, a stocky figure with bright blue eyes that looked directly at any man with which he did business. After the election, he worked hard to clear out those residents uninterested in obeying the law. When the Apaches raided local ranches, he did not hesitate to follow their trail. He quickly gained a reputation as a tough and honest sheriff. Only after he completed a second term was John allowed to return to the ranch he had purchased four years earlier.

The San Bernardino ranch had not fared well during the years of abandonment. When the wagon bearing John's wife, Violetta Slaughter, topped the low rise overlooking the springs, she saw the site for the first time. She exclaimed,

"As we came out of the Sulphur Springs Valley and came into a pass in the Silver Creek range, we looked east and south to the Guadalupes in New Mexico and into the distant blue of Old Mexico. Two streams watered the valley. It was beautiful and it was ours."

Slaughter built a spacious adobe home a short distance from the border with Mexico. Two thirds of his ranch lay on the other side of the international border. He drilled down into the springs, until he hit water at 550 feet. Slaughter placed a pipe into the spring and water surged upward over the lip of the pipe nearly eight feet above ground level, creating an artesian well.

The San Bernardino Wildlife Refuge spreads across the horizon on both sides of the international border. Twelve ponds and 14 wells are fed by an artesian aquifer. The ponds are used as a hatchery for native Yaqui Top Minnow and Yaqui Chub.

    Artesian conditions are created when stress deep within the earth exerts pressure on rock layers above. When a release point is created, such as an artesian well or spring, the water flows upward without aid from a pump. When Slaughter drilled into the aquifer, that pressure found a release and the the water shot up through the pipe like a fountain. No pumps are needed to pull the water upward due to the artesian pressure. Today, a pump is used to transfer water from the pond to the corrals and big gun sprinklers in the pasture.

    Jennifer Varan, a biologist with the Coronado Forest Service, has described one artesian location near Clifton. She tells of standing in a marshy area, feeling the ground vibrate under her feet from the pressure of the water seeking an outlet to the surface.

    Slaughter developed two large ponds on the ranch: one in a wash north of the headquarters, the other the house pond providing water to the house and livestock. He drained the marsh around the springs and placed 500 acres under irrigation, planting wheat, barley, beans and cotton. The last of these is a water hungry crop. He developed two other smaller ponds and drilled 10 wells across the ranch's 65,000 acres. In the evenings the Louisiana bullfrogs he brought to the house pond croaked into the twilight. Yaqui catfish provided meals other than the beef and mutton from his ranch.

* The Tombstone Epitaph, March 1933

In the 1930's water sold for $5 a gallon in Phoenix. During the restoration of the ranch, old glass bottles were recovered that were once part of the trading over the border: Water for gasoline.

John and Violetta Slaughter lived on the ranch until his death in 1922. After his death, the ranch passed from owner to owner until purchased in trust by the Nature Conservancy. The United States Game and Wildlife Service purchased the land around the spring in 1982 intending to develop a hatchery for the endangered Yaqui chub, Yaqui topminnow and Yaqui catfish. Today, the Johnson Historical Museum of the Southwest owns 131 acres with the ranch house, the house pond and outbuildings, with a bit of pasture to continue the tradition that John Slaughter began so successfully. The remainder of the US portion of San Bernardino is still held by the Fish and Wildlife Service.

Entering the San Bernardino ranch, massive cottonwoods fill the horizon. The largest would require two to three people, stretching their arms outward to encircle the trunk. The size of the cottonwoods speaks of the water that lies just under the surface. Stepping out of the car, the sound of water rushing from deep underground harmonizes with the wind stirring the leaves of the cottonwoods. Living in Arizona I am unused to hearing the sound of water moving beneath the earth's surface. Glancing around, I could not see a stream that might produce the sound. This is the soundtrack of an artesian spring.

I moved up a slope through the shade of the cottonwoods to stand on the edge of the pond. The pond, at a depth of 20 feet, is much deeper than I expected. Six springs release sixty to one hundred gallons a minute through fractures in

The home pond on the Slaughter Ranch drops to 22 feet, lined with malpais rock. As an artesian spring, none of the water is pumped to the surface but rises from pressure over the the aquifer. A deep layer of clay holds the aquifer in the rock layers.

the rock beneath the pond. The dark surface reflects the blue sky. A slight breeze lifted the leaves of the cottonwood and I could not imagine a more pleasant place to be in southern Arizona than in the middle of Slaughter's Ranch. A bench overlooking the wind-stirred surface of the pond invites visitors to sit and stay a while.

West of the pond is the adobe ranch house. For an 1800-era house, this home is spacious. Behind the home are the outbuildings where those employed on the ranch did the work required in caring for the ranch hands and Slaughter's family. A quarter mile east of the ranch, one lone spring released warm water where Violetta Slaughter and the other women bathed in the evenings.

We spent some time with the caretakers for the property. After arriving to open the gate to the ranch, they were busy with the goats and other livestock. As the goats streamed out of their pen, one worked his way around me. Preoccupied with the conversation, I jumped as I felt a little nip to the back of my leg. The goat had my attention.

I peered down at a rusty iron fence that marks the border. The fence is constructed out of iron rails used by the railroad that once ran from Douglas to the mines in Mexico. I wondered if those who cross the border illegally would see the ranch as a promising passage due to the springs.

When the Dunns became caretakers for the property, people were slipping across the border to wander through the buildings before heading north. Fred spoke with the men who worked for him. He was fairly certain they might know the smugglers who were transporting the immigrants to the border. He promised that if they would respect the property and take their activities to another part of the border, he in turn would not cause trouble for them. However, if they continued to smuggle people across the ranch, he would make their lives difficult. Fred has not had trouble with illegal crossings since making that promise.

One never knows what they might encounter on the border. He packs a large caliber pistol on his hip. He told us the story of smugglers with two new trucks, big trucks with powerful engines. Just as during the 1940-era of Prohibition, these men were racing along back roads trying to allude the Border patrol. The Fish and Wildlife Service had just finished building a beautiful new dock, extending out over one of the ponds on the property below the ranch. In the moonlight, the smugglers mistook the dock for a bridge. In a moment, both trucks were airborne and sank into the pond, effectively ending the pursuit! The soggy smugglers were apprehended with the seizure of a large shipment of marijuana.

Otherwise, life is quiet at Slaughter's Ranch.

The water table has dropped since John Slaughter first sank a pipe into the springs. Water no longer erupts from an eight-foot tall pipe. The flow of water is now controlled through a web of pipes, fittings and gauges. Unlike the border at Nogales, there are no large towns pumping water from this part of the aquifer. As we rolled back toward Douglas I marveled at the size of an aquifer required to support such a large desert spring.

As I think about Arizona's southern border with Mexico, we learn from the historical record that the springs allowed people to live in an arid environment. They moved from one perennial source of water to the next, whether springs, river or rock basins filled with run-off from recent storms.

A second pond on the ranch sat in Black Draw, on the edge of an ancient volcanic intrusion. Black Draw has alluvial sediments overlaying older conglomerate layers. At one time, the water lay just 20 feet below the surface of Black Draw.

Water is the foundation for life in the Sonoran and Chihuahua deserts.

Water by the Road

Once the United States acquired the southwestern territory, Lieutentant Edward Beale was tasked with building a wagon route along the 35th Parallel across the Territory of New Mexico in 1856. There were few roads throughout the southwest, mostly just Native trails. With the Civil War behind them, settlers were eager to learn the potential of this new territory.

The route, which became known as the Beale Wagon Road, began in Fort Smith, Arkansas and stretched 1,240 miles to the Colorado River. Lt. Beale was concerned about how horses and mules would travel in the arid southwest. He conceived a plan to import 22 camels with their drivers from Syria to carry some of the supplies required by his crew of 50 to 100 men. The bulk of the equipment would still be transported by mule-drawn wagons. Undoubtably, the experiment had the potential to make camels a mainstay in the southwest in the years that followed. The animals did very well over the sandy plains. The malpais or rough volcanic rock did not injure the animals' flat feet. The one flaw in the plan came from the mule drivers who passionately hated the camels.

Lt. Beale knew that the success of the road depended on the availability of the wood for campfires, grass for grazing and water for the thirsty livestock and travelers. Two years earlier Captain Amiel Whipple had traveled along the 35th parallel, recording a number of springs and water sources. The springs and streams lay around 20 miles apart, a distance easily traveled within a day, maybe two if the terrain became difficult.

In 1857, after crossing the Rio Grande River, Beale's expedition arrived at a spring called Jacob's Well, located north of the Zuni pueblos. Jacob's Well was described as a conical depression with near vertical walls. This may have been a sink hole. A trail descended along the wall of the depression to a deep pool of water. In his report Lt. Beale described the spring:

"The traveler, following the trail on a level plain, comes suddenly to the brink of a perfectly circular hole of about a quarter of a mile in circumference, and a hundred yards in almost perpendicular descent. The sides of this hole slope very steeply nearly to the bottom, where a basin of apparently very great depth, and about sixty yards in circumference, completed the picture. Around the edges of this pool grow rushes and a few small willows and cedars. The water is agreeable to the taste, though a little brackish, and in

Navajo Spring

Arizona was first recognized as part of the Territory of New Mexico. However, the residents of the western half of the territory began to realize they did not share the goals and values of the Hispanic population in the eastern half and petitioned for independent status as the Arizona territory. In 1863, President Abraham Lincoln appointed John Goodwin to be Arizona's first territorial governor. Goodwin traveled west to Santa Fe, then departed for the new territory, following the Beale Wagon Road. He intended to tour what few towns existed in the territory and settle on a location for the capitol.

When his party arrived at Navajo Spring, Goodwin was sworn into office. He then began to appoint the officials that would lead the territorial government. One of his first acts was to renounce the legal system inherited from New Mexico which was based on Mexico's system of peonage.

After establishing the capitol at a site on Granite Creek near the town of Prescott, he did not remain in Arizona for long. When the next election cycle rolled around, he defeated Charles Poston for the position of territorial delegate to Congress. Over the next four decades, thousands of emigrants with herds of sheep and cattle stopped at Navajo Spring as they moved west.

it are quite a number of fish. It is only accessible by one trail, which follows the nearly precipitous sides, winding gradually down."

As one gazes across the desert plain from the I-40 exit at the Sanders, the plain is flat and it is possible to understand how a circular depression might go undiscovered until an explorer passed within a few feet. Today no trace of the depression remains. Sand in alliance with the dropping aquifer and gravity have filled in Jacob's Well.

Leaving Jacob's Well, Beale's expedition moved on to Navajo Springs which is south of the community of Houck. Baldwin Mollhausen kept a diary of their travels and described the marshy cienega.

"From this remarkable lake, or pond [Jacob's Well], we passed on in a more northerly direction, and had scarcely gone six miles before we came to the fresh spring [Navajo Springs] that had been mentioned, and immediately made preparations for resting

and passing the night there. The water was gushing out of the ground in several places, but instead of the various runnels uniting into a brook, they overflowed the nearest low ground and transferred into a marsh, in the small pools of which, however, we found abundance of excellent water for ourselves and our cattle."

The description of water gushing out of the ground might indicate that this spring had artesian qualities. The outflow did not form a stream as the ground is relatively flat in this region. Instead the water created a marsh with small pools of water.

This entire region was once a shallow lake bed covering much of northeastern Arizona and northwestern New Mexico. Layers of sand, silt and mud settled in the waters of this ancient sea, creating the Bidahochi formation that overlies an impervious layer of Mancos shale. Both Jacob's Well and Navajo spring emerged from the Bidahochi formation. The Bidahochi aquifer overlies the much deeper Coconino aquifer. Looking to the north, beyond I-40, runoff from a small range of hills would contribute to the aquifer. Wells in the area east of the spring may supply five to twenty gallons of water a minute. This would be in keeping with early descriptions of the spring.

Today, a large water tank sits at the site and the water has been diverted through a pipe into the tank. The rusty structure gives no hint of the history that once took place at Navajo Spring.

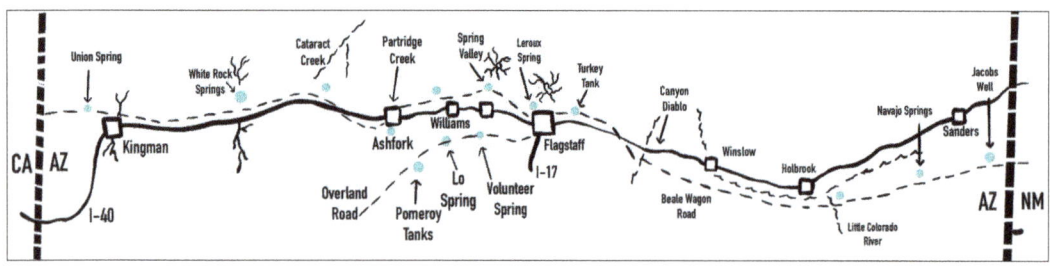

The Route of the Beale Wagon Road

Moving westward, the men traveled through what is now the Petrified Forest. Lt. Beale described their route as relatively flat and easy to travel. They reached the valley of the Little Colorado River and camped near the junction with Canyon Diablo.

West of Canyon Diablo the land surface begins to rise toward the San Francisco Peaks. The Coconino Plateau is a region that consists of a thin layer of volcanic rock overlaying thick layers of limestone and sandstone. Three large aquifers underlie this region: The Navajo, the Dakota and the Coconino. Together the three are thought to hold around 508 million acre feet of water and are the source for the larger springs and wells.

As the Beale party approached the San Francisco Peaks, they came to a deep pool lined with volcanic rocks on the edge of the San Francisco Wash. This

Low water at Turkey Tank

large wash cuts a wide swath through a bed of cinder cones. The cinder cones are the remnants of volcanic activity that overlay a thick layer of Kaibab sandstone. Standing on the rim of the ravine visitors can easily identify the lava intrusion.

One of Beale's men shot a turkey and so the spring was named Turkey Tank. This spring was a reliable source of water for the ancient Sinagua and for native traders and hunting parties traveling through the region.

Upon arriving at the site, I questioned how cattle or horses could make their way through the abrasive volcanic rock down to the pool of water. At the time of Beale's arrival, the pool was more extensive and deeper. A footpath descends the south side of the ravine. On the west end of the tank, a low cement wall might once have held back the water that streamed along the wash. On the ridge above the tank, cars roar past enroute to the Navajo community of Leupp.

From Turkey Tanks, the Beale party traveled west toward the base of the San Francisco Peaks. In the 1970s, Jack Smith researched the route of the Beale Party and determined that Linda Vista Road in Flagstaff was built over the route the Beale party followed. At this point Lt. Beale and his men would have found the task of road building a bit more arduous. No longer could they leave a set of tracks across a brush covered plain. Now they dug and pushed volcanic boulders to the side of a ten-foot wide track.

They came to a long valley on the western exposure of the San Francisco Peaks with a series of springs that we call Old Town, Clark, McMillian, Big Leroux and Little Leroux. Within a few years of the expedition, Brigham Young,

Clark Spring: The Flagstaff City Pond

A rancher named Clark was the first permanent resident in what is now Flagstaff. He built a cabin at a fresh water spring and emigrants began stopping to re-fill their barrels and ask about the road west.

The spring named after him is no longer visible due to being submerged by the Flagstaff City Pond. At one time the flow along the Rio de Flag, a channel which contains the spring, may have been significant. Verna Castleberry, a long-time resident of Flagstaff, once recalled swimming her horse across the stream in the 1920's when the stream swelled with spring runoff.

In the 1970's Jim Davidson taught at the Flagstaff Junior High School located on a rise above the spring. With all the traffic along the wash, the ground had become more of a swamp with a small stream trickling through the mud. Jim thought the area might make a great city park with a pond as the centerpiece where his biology classes could do hands-on learning. A city-wide campaign led to the creation of the pond lined with rushes and a small dock. Ducks and mud hens drop in on the quiet water as fishermen cast a line from the shore.

The spring is submerged, its history forgotten. The pond's water level remain fairly constant, assisted by the silent flow of Clark spring and runoff down the Rio de Flag.

the leader of the Latter Day Saints, would send his followers to lay claim to every spring and ferry crossing in northern Arizona. Due to the threat from native tribes, the Latter Day Saints would build a small wooden palisade below Leroux Spring in 1877, for which 'Fort Valley' is named.

The Rio de Flag, a seasonal stream, flows out of Fort Valley. The headwaters of the stream, along with several springs, lie on the slopes of the San Francisco Peaks. The springs found in Fort Valley are the markers of the aquifer's flow. Dr. Abe Springer and his students at Northern Arizona University have studied the springs, monitoring how the seasons effect their flow.

When settlers first came to the Valley, they found the water table to be just 10 feet below the surface in some locations. The water spilling from the springs along with rich top soil made this a desirable location.

Big Leroux Spring

Big Leroux is one of the springs. When Major Amiel Whipple's party first reached the spring, the account reads, *"After traveling about seven miles, we reached a permanent spring that poured from a hillside and was lost in the grassy plain below. In honor of the guide it was called Leroux's spring. It is the same to which he conducted Captain Sitgreaves two years since, but by a different route, passing around the north and the western base of the mountain."*

A week later the account records, *"The height above Leroux's Spring was found to be 4,673 feet, making it about 12,000 feet above the level of the sea. At noon, the temperature of the spring, where it issues from the hill-side, was measured. The immersed thermometer read 48.8 degrees; 3.2 degrees higher than the surrounding*

Spring box

atmosphere. That is probably the mean temperature of the place. The water pours, in several streams, down the ravine, producing a fringe of green herbage."

The settlers in the region were quick to tap the spring as a perennial source of water. A small dam was built in the valley below Big Leroux as a collection point but never held much water. As Flagstaff struggled to find a reliable water supply, water from Big Leroux and Little Leroux springs was shipped in barrels by wagon to the small settlement. If a household or business required their water barrel to be filled, a white cloth was hung on their porch or fence post.

Historically, the spring was said to produce about 40,000 gallons in a day. More modern observation has indicated that the flow fluctuates and the spring may produce from seven to 37 gallons a minute. Like the springs that flow from the inner basin of the peaks, the precipitation that falls on the peaks percolates down through the cinders, preserving the quality of the water. Due to the porosity of the soil and the shallow depth of the aquifer, the water must emerge quickly or be lost to any modern use.

In time, the spring was capped and diverted into a large cement spring box, shown above. The hillside flow was reduced to a trickle. In 2013, the US Forest Service made the decision to allow much of the water to once again flow down the hillside. At a second box below the original spring box, a drain valve is left open. With the current drought, a trickle with pockets of water remain on the hillside below the spring.

Gone are the days when a spring of this size might be allowed to flow down the hillside without restriction. Like Big Leroux, most of the large springs in the state have been diverted for private use.

Little Leroux spring is located south of Big Leroux. The water has been diverted through a pipe for use at the Experimental Station on US Highway 180.

McMillan Spring, now renamed **Coyote Spring**, it is located on the property of the Museum of Northern Arizona and flows intermittently. The spring is protected by a large cement box. Nearby, a small root cellar dug with a weathered door, was dug by an early settler. After snow melt or adequate summer rains, spring water flows across the hillside to Highway 180. The stream channel is marked by cattails and brush. Game cameras have captured a wide range of wildlife using the spring but the most admired are the mule deer that startle drivers along the approach to the nearby assisted living facility.

    Flagstaff no longer relies on Big Leroux spring as the town did in the first two decades of existence. Both the springs are important to the wildlife that come to the water at dusk. Larger animals can drink, standing at the edge of the containment box. The restored flow along the hillside allows smaller mammals to access the small pools of water without tumbling into the spring box and drowning. Lush fern and wild flowers are returning to the slopes of the small canyon. Standing below the stream, there is a sense of balance returning as we watch the water released once again.

    Returning to the Beale Wagon Road, those in the wagon trains that followed Beale's Road often spent several days resting in the valley before moving toward their destination. Moving west, the region around the community of Parks renders an amazing number of springs which must have been welcomed by trail- worn travelers. Today, an area just north of Parks is called Spring Valley, a stop recorded on the Beale Wagon Road.

A ridge of large basalt boulders at Laws Spring reminds us that volcanic intrusions are often the conduit for water from underlying sedimentary layers.

Laws Spring was the next stop after Spring Valley. One member of the party, a tombstone engraver, recorded the name on a large basalt boulder. Even today the small pool is muddy from a herd of cattle, reminding us of the herds that traveled the wagon route.

After Laws Spring, finding water became more tenuous. John Udell was a member of the first wagon train to follow the road before it had been improved. He writes of stopping at both Partridge Creek and at a deep canyon with steep walls which may have been Cataract Canyon.

Beyond Ashfork, the plateau drops in elevation, the landscape changing to a dry, rocky plain cut by deep canyons. White Rock Spring in Truxton Canyon is mentioned in both the Beale party record and by John Udell. While driving Route 66 into Truxton, observant travelers note the tall cottonwoods that line the

Old Town Spring

The AT&T Railroad laid track along 35th Parallel through Flagstaff. Old Town, a community of loggers was first built at the end of a dirt road that parallelled the tracks. Early residents drew water from the spring. The spring's flow varies, depending on precipitation.

Many Flagstaff residents have forgotten that a perched aquifer lies under the ridge lining the west end of Flagstaff. The spring reminds them of its existence when water begins to emerge in the basements and along the foundations of homes built on the slopes above Old Town Spring and neighborhood park.

canyon bottoms in the region. Cottonwood are one of the markers for ground water in a desert region.

The last spring mentioned is in Union Pass between Kingman and Bullhead City. After passing through the mountains that line the eastern edge of the Colorado, the Beale crew came to the brown waters of the Colorado River.

Lt. Edward Beale returned to the Beale Wagon Road in 1859. His crew of men worked to refine the road and the location of water sources travelers would depend on. Over the next 25 years, the springs along the Beale Wagon Road were a lifeline leading the travelers west to California and a new life.

The Springs Along the Overland Trail

In 1863, gold was discovered along the Hassayampa River near Prescott. As with other gold strikes, prospectors were eager to reach this new strike. Some of the would-be prospectors came north from the Southern Overland Route. Others looked for a route turning south off the Beale Wagon Road.

The 85-mile Overland Trail from Flagstaff to Prescott was used heavily between 1863 and 1882 and is not to be confused with the transcontinental route by the same name. The road south began at Old Town Spring and followed the base of the ridge, passing Tunnel Spring to A-1 Mountain. Further west lay Volunteer Spring at Camp Navajo in Bellemont. Driving south from the entrance of Camp Navajo at Bellemont, the road follows the shoreline of a large pond nestled in Volunteer Wash. I joined a group from the Arizona Hydrological Society standing on the edge of the wash, a group as Dr. Randy Wilkerson described the faults that cross this section of Camp Navajo.

Under the intrusions of volcanic deposits that once crept across the landscape is a layer of Kaibab limestone. As discussed in Part 1, water will create an underground network of cracks, caverns and sinkholes called a karst in limestone. There is indeed a karst under Camp Navajo and this limestone network is responsible for the abundance of springs at Camp Navajo. The Bellemont fault runs south to north across Camp Navajo, giving a vertical path for the water held in the limestone. Bellemont and Volunteer springs flow out of the aquifer along the fault, once providing a source of water for travelers along the Overland Road and later for Camp Navajo. The water still flows today, with land owners in the area pulling up to a spigot to fill water tanks in the back of their pickups or trailers. As the shallow wells in the vicinity go dry in mid-summer, residents rely on Bellemont Spring. In the last four decades, the landowners faced a possible loss of access to this water for several years due to drought.

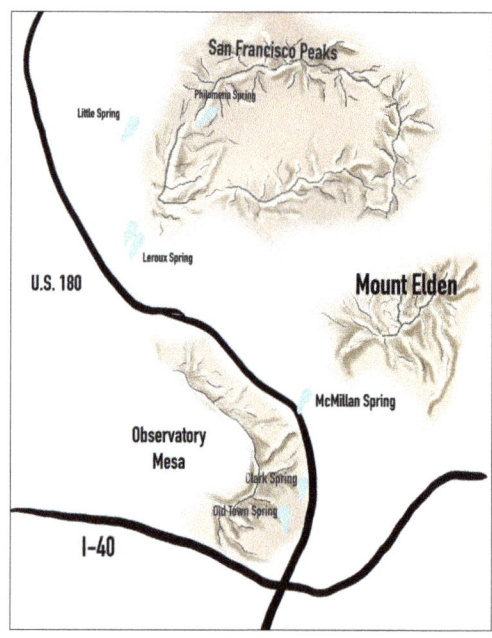

When the subdivision was erected north of the freeway, the corporation building the subdivision was required by the 1980 Arizona Water Code to show they could supply water to homeowners without relying on Volunteer Spring. Nine wells were drilled, two drawing from a shallow aquifer. The remainder drop 2,000 feet and deeper, drawing water from the Coconino aquifer. The drilling rigs hit water at 1,400 feet with one well producing around 150 gallons a minute.

In 2019, bulldozers began clearing another section for a new subdivision. Once again, neighboring land owners are expressing concern that increasing the draw down will impact their shallow wells and the aquifer that feeds Volunteer and Bellemont's smaller springs.

Bellemont lies along the western end of a series of ridges that begin east of Mormon Mountain. The precipitation that falls along the ridges actively feeds the Coconino aquifer. The aquifer moves north from this crescent to springs where it is released. Wells drilled 20 miles west of Bellemont indicate that the Coconino aquifer is starting to dry along the far western edge. This is believed to be due to

In 1882, the AT&T railroad laid rails through Flagstaff for a transcontinental route. Tunnel spring was directed into a large tank where the steam-driven engines could refill their tenders. Today, years of drought have diminished the shallow aquifer to a mere trickle, flowing in the early months of the year.

the demands on the aquifer and the lack of replenishment in a drought that has lasted over twenty years.

Returning to the route of the Overland Road, after leaving Volunteer spring, travelers turned southwest, crossing Garland Prairie to the rim of Sycamore Canyon. This wilderness canyon slices through the Mogollon Rim, a massive uplift stretching 200 miles across Arizona. The Mogollon Rim stands 2,000 feet above the land surface at its base, exposing layers of Kaibab limestone and Coconino sandstone.

Dow Spring and LO Spring lie just below the rim along LO Canyon, a shallow wash that drains into Sycamore Canyon. The two springs are fed by a perched aquifer. At Dow Spring the water trickles from a metal pipe protruding from the canyon wall. On the rim above are the timbers of small cabin along an old rail bed, left from the days when rail cars brought ore out of the mines near Prescott. As the summer lengthens, the stream from this hillside spring begins to falter and soon the pool in the wash evaporates, leaving only the stain of standing water. In late spring water lilies float on the surface of the pond and damsel flies

Dow Spring

flit across the water seeking their next meal. The spring is named for James Dow, with Garland Prairie named after his partner William Garland.

From Dow Springs, a short walk leads to LO, a rheocrene spring. After a wet winter, the pools spread across the floor of the wash. By late summer, when Dow Spring has stopped flowing, LO Spring still maintains a series of pools along the canyon bottom. In 2019, the reeds lining the ponds reached 10 feet overhead.

The surface of the pond was nearly obscured by water lilies. Knee-high, lush grass filled the small wash. For a traveler in the 1800s, this would have been a welcomed rest stop.

A larger chain of pools awaited travelers at the next spring along the Overland Trail at Pomeroy Tanks. Basalt boulders line the rim of the wash. Precipitation drains from the surrounding meadows into the shallow canyon and over Sycamore Falls each spring. As the surface dries, water remains in the pools fed by small rheocrene springs rising out of a shallow aquifer overlaid by a layer of basalt.

Knowing the pools were perennial made this a reliable stop on the Overland Trail. As I first made my way to a pool in the 1990's, I wondered how the drovers brought wagons over the basalt rim. No trace remains of a stock trail, though one must have existed.

When I returned to Pomeroy Tanks as part of my research, my husband accompanied me, following the display on his i-pad. And therein lay some

LO Spring & lilly pads

confusion! He was quite certain the marker indicated the spring lay a half mile further and I insisted that the upper pool was our destination. As we wandered along the rim, we encountered another tank, followed by another. It became clear that Pomeroy is a series of tanks along the drainage above Sycamore Falls. With each successive pool, the canyon deepens and becomes a bit wilder.

We stopped at a pool at the base of dark basalt cliffs wrapped in brush and vine. From the rim, we could see grassy meadows surrounding each pool. We picked our way down a steep slope through basalt boulders to a meadow with lush grass. Overhead, a log spanned the distance between rock walls. The log may have fallen from the rim or been carried by high water which made me wonder about the water that flows down this watercourse.

Beyond the pools the drainage drops over Sycamore Falls between cliffs of accordioned rock. Climbers suspended from incredibly slender lines seek tiny crevices for a finger hold as they scale the cliffs. There are other isolated springs in the depths of this massive canyon and we will consider three of these in talking about a hermit that found refuge in this wild place.

The Overland Trail continued west to Lockett Spring before turning south. Today we can drive the historic trail toward Prescott by following South Road out of Williams. After the pavement turns to dirt, the road passes through a corner of one of the largest pine forests in the world before the landscape turns to rugged grasslands.

Volcanic rocks speak of a conduit to the earth's surface for Pomeroy Springs, rising out of a limestone karst.

As we drive the rocky surface, we can better appreciate the skill of the men who laced reins through their fingers and drove their teams from one spring to the next, taking time to stop and water their animals.

Pipe Springs

The Beale Road and Overland Road were not the only two historic routes across northern Arizona that were dependent on the springs. In 1821, Mexico gained independence from Spain. Under Spanish rule, the settlements in California and New Mexico had been forced to communicate and trade directly with Mexico

City rather than each other. Free from Spanish oversight, traders began to seek a route west from Santa Fe, New Mexico to the settlements on the Pacific coast. Two Spanish friars had already attempted such to find a route north of the Grand Canyon, but turned back, daunted by the harsh canyon lands.

In 1829, Antonio Armijo established the first trade route from Santa Fe to the San Gabriel Mission in Los Angeles. His party included 50 men and 100 pack animals. Traveling north from the Delores River, he crossed the Four Corners region to the the Colorado River and the ford known as Crossing of the Fathers. After crossing the Kanab Plateau, he came to a cluster of springs in the northwest corner of our state on December 15, 1829.

He called the springs Agua de la Vieja or the Water of the Old Woman. The site is now Pipe Springs National Monument. From Agua de la Vieja, Armijo crossed the Unikaret Plateau to the Virgin River and turned south toward the Colorado River before crossing the Mohave desert.

The springs emerge at the base of the Vermillion Cliffs along the west side of the Sevier Fault. The groundwater flows south through fractures till it is blocked by fault movement.

Archeological evidence shows the spring was used by the Anasazi, and then by the Paiute tribe, for hundreds of years before the Spanish arrived. While these tribes were primarily hunters and gathers, they did plant some crops near the springs. However, by the 1800s the Navajos had entered the territory and were competing with the Paiutes for the region's fragile resources. When Armijo's party reached the spring the land was covered by tall grass supported by a delicate ecosystem. Pipe Springs became popular with traders following the Armijo Route.

Brigham Young and his followers stumbled out of the Wasatch Mountains into the valley of the Great Salt Lake in 1848. Jacob Hamblin, one of Young's favorite scouts, had gained a reputation for his knowledge of the southwest territory and his skill in negotiating with the Navajo. In 1858, following Young's assignment, Hamblin led a party of men to explore the territory beyond the Grand Canyon and to learn more of the Hopi in their villages on the high mesas. Pipe Springs was the only consistent source of water for a hundred miles, between the settlements in Utah and Kanab Creek. Hamblin built several small dugouts near the springs to provide shelter and establish a claim to the spring.

A year later, Brigham Young accompanied Jacob Hamblin to the springs. As Young surveyed the water tumbling from the rocky slope, he announced that such a fine flow of good water must be protected. At the time, the springs were flowing at a rate of 50 gallons per minute. Marching up the hillside to the main outlet, he paced off the perimeter of a fort to be built over the spring. Young could not have known that the Sevier fault ran directly under his feet. Considering the historic building still stands 148 years later, the fault seems to be stable.

Dr. James Whitmore and his partner Robert McIntyre followed the explorer

Winsor Castle at Pipe Springs National Monument

to the springs. They brought the first herd of cattle to the grasslands and built a small dugout of juniper logs. In January 1866, a Navajo raiding party found Whitmore and McIntyre searching for lost cattle. Whitmore's 11-year-old son was the only survivor of the raid, hiding in the dugout.

In November 1869, drovers brought 500 head of cattle, 500 horses and mules along with 2,000 Merino sheep to graze the waist-high grass that covered the plains around the spring. In 1884, more sheep arrived, escaping a severe drought in California.

Anson Winsor arrived in 1870 and began cutting Kaibab sandstone from the hillside to build two buildings facing each other across a wagon yard. The Navajo raids had begun to subside so the size of the fort was decreased to 68 by 44 feet. When the fort was completed in 1872, heavy wooden gates were installed across each end of the courtyard between the two buildings. The fort was intended as a fall-back position if a raiding party threatened the settlers again. The Paiute were no longer considered a threat since only 100 members of the tribe had survived the conflict known as the Black Hawk War. They remained on good terms with the settlers.

Anson Winsor and his wife were the first managers of the agricultural station. To assist the family, young LDS men and women arrived, taking up residence. The cattle soon multiplied, and by 1874 nearly 400 head of cattle grazed the plain. The young women would milk 100 head each day - by hand. The milk was brought to one of the lower rooms of the fort.

How the water was used in the dairy operations at ranch makes this one of my favorite springs in Arizona. As described, the fort was built directly over the main spring. The water rising from Main Spring under the north side was channeled through a pipe under the courtyard into a long stone trough in a room on the lower level of the south half of fort. On the far end of the trough, a second pipe releases the water to a pond below the fort. The water flowing through the trough helped to cool the room to around 50 degrees which must have been a relief during the warm summers. The women would have had little time to enjoy the relief.

Within the 'cheese' room, the young women would pour the milk from the dairy cows into a large vat where it was heated to 90 degrees. Rennet, an enzyme, was added causing the milk to separate into curds as part of the process for producing cheese. As the milk thickened, the mixture was poured into wooden frames to cure.

Along with cheese, the women also produced 60 to 70 pounds of butter each day. Their method was ingenious as they tied the containers to rocking chairs and set several of the Winsor's 11 children to rocking back and forth, churning the fresh milk. The butter and cheese along with fresh meat was shipped to the community of Saint George to be sold in the stores, thus providing funds for the ranch.

A stone trough carries spring water, piped from a spring below the fort. The water was used in cheese making in the 1800's.

In 1879, the Pipe Springs Cattle Company was absorbed into the Canaan Cooperative Growing Company out of Saint George. While appearing to be independent businesses, both properties were part of the estate of Brigham Young.

Edwin and Flora Woolley were the next managers of the ranch, adding an additional 2,269 head of cattle with 162 horses and mules. With such a large herd the ranch employed 75 men and women. Flora Woolley was quick to put her signature on the building, insisting that windows be added to each room looking into the courtyard. She also insisted on a stove, refusing to work over an outdoor fire cooking for her family and the ranch hands. In time, Flora, herself a second wife, would shelter other plural wives within the walls of the fort as the US government began a campaign against polygamy.

Under the management of both companies, the fort was designated a tithing ranch with the task of supplying dairy, meat and hides to the workers building the Saint George Latter-Day Saint Temple. As they looked to expand farming at the springs beyond the grain crops, the Woolleys hoped to grow both sugarcane and cotton. Sugar was still a rare commodity in the west and the cotton would have been ginned, spun and woven into fabric for shirts and dresses. These crops are water hungry and would have placed an even greater demand on the springs.

With the expansion of the ranch and the years of excessive grazing by large herds of cattle, the plains surrounding Pipe Springs began to suffer. The herds of cattle and sheep, particularly Merino sheep, grazed the grass down to the dirt. In such a dry climate without adequate rainfall, the eco-system could not recover. In the 1930s Leonard Heaton, the Park manager, would make an attempt to re-seed an area near the springs with native grass. The attempt failed.

In 1885, Congress passed the Edmunds-Tucker Act which outlawed polygamy, also ended the Perpetual Emmigration Fund that brought converts to the United States. The law forced the church to sell property valued over $50,000 which included Pipe Springs.

After a succession of owners, the United States Park Service purchased the springs and the surrounding 40 acres in 1923. The springs and sandstone structure known as Winsor Castle became a National Monument. Over the next decade, the demand for water from the local ranchers, the fort and the Paiutes began to increase and there was some question as to who owned the rights to the springs both at Pipe Spring and Moccasin.

The Pipe Springs Monument is surrounded by the Paiute Reservation with the small town of Moccasin, seven miles north of the Monument. The Paiutes were becoming increasingly concerned about the amount of water they received from neighboring Moccasin spring. They believed that the water was being diverted to the farms and homes of white families living in Moccasin, leaving them an insufficient supply. The white families retorted that that their farming was a beneficial use of the water. If the tribe's claim to the water was given precedence, the ranchers were afraid that they would lose the access to the water from the springs for their livestock. In 1933, a compact was signed, dividing the water between the Paiutes, the National Monument and the town of Moccasin. This compact remains in effect to this day.

Prior to the compact, the flow of the springs was measured. The historic spring, located under the fort, was flowing at 5.67 gallons a minute. A second large spring 25 yards off the southwest corner of the fort released 27.77 gallons a minute. Tunnel Spring was producing 7.7 gallons per minute while a small seep was under a quart a minute. Since the arrival of the LDS settlers, flow had dropped 50 gallons to just over 40 gallons a minute.

In 1972, the Park Service agreed to finance the drilling of a well with a water system that would distribute water to the Paiute tribe. The first attempt in

A spring fed pond at Pipe Springs National Mounument.

Two Mile Wash did not produce water. A second attempt was made, drilling into the bedrock surrounding the Park and the drill rig hit water at 205 feet.

By the late 1970s the Park Service noted that the flow from the springs had begun to slow and the decline continued into the 1980s. The Park Service began to consider rehabilitating Tunnel Spring. They knew the tunnel into the spring had been covered, but as work began in 1987, they were surprised to find the extent of the labor that had been done.

First, the soil covering the tunnel was removed. This revealed a 90-foot channel covered by cedar and juniper boards, supported by 26 braces. After removing the boards and braces, they found the channel was six feet high by four feet wide. Water was found in the upper 60 feet of the channel. No water appeared at the end of the channel.

Upon reaching the rock face at the high end of the channel, the Park Service found that a tunnel had been excavated into the sandstone for another 50 feet. This passage was only four feet high and two feet wide. Consider for a moment what it would have taken to dig such a tunnel with hand tools while hunched over with little room to either side. A two-inch pipe had been laid along the channel to divert water to a pond located above the fort.

Near the entrance to the sandstone tunnel, the Park Service employees found the skeleton of a horse laying in the channel. Apparently the horse had gone missing but the ranch hands failed to find the animal in the narrow channel and the horse was unable to climb out. The skeleton, along with thick roots and sediment was removed. Water once again flowed from Tunnel Spring but the flow remained greatly diminished from what had been when first discovered by the Spanish and later managed by LDS settlers.

Then, in 1999, the flow of water from Main Spring located under the fort stopped. A study was done trying to determine the cause of de-watering. The hydrologists concluded that the aquifer was dropping due to the number of wells in the area pulling water for agricultural and home use. Tunnel spring, located west of the ponds, continued to produce 11 gallons per minute. The Park Service determined to divert this water into the channel that once flowed from Main spring.

In 2006 a hydrological study was done and scientists learned that there were actually two springs rather than three. The spring southwest of the fort was serving as a second outlet for the historic spring location under the fort. Both reached the surface along the same conduit. Tunnel Spring remained separate from the two at the fort. Cabin Spring is now classified as a wet meadow. The study found that the springs were supported by a shallow aquifer with a circumference of about seven miles. This does not leave much of a margin for a large draw down of the water table.

Looking at the plains surrounding the Park, we now understand that the vast herds stripped the bunch grass from the top, leaving it unprotected. The region is now semi-arid, sparsely populated with juniper and pinyon pine, rabbit and skunk brush. The wind lifts the dust from the parched ground and drives the grit across the plains. More wells have been dug and more water drained from the aquifer.

When the personnel at The Springs Institute talk about the state of a spring, they qualify whether a spring has been completely or partially disrupted from its natural state by human activity. Pipe Springs has been diverted, disrupted and managed for over one hundred years. The natural riparian zone has been eliminated, replaced by two pools of water lined with rock.

The question remains: is it better to leave a spring in the natural state or to divert the spring for our benefit? A related question: does the right to live in this arid climate outweigh the value of what is best for the natural resource. The Paiute maintain small gardens while communities along Arizona's border with Utah continue to grow. If the springs are to survive, harsh measures would have to be taken to preserve the aquifers and limit the draw down. Tunnel Spring may disappear just as the historic spring did in 1999. Pipe Springs could very well become a showplace without a spring to show.

Nail Canyon

The farming and ranching activity at Pipe Springs encourged settlers to move east. Unlike the grasslands of the Kanab Plateau, the Kaibab Plateau is covered with lush forests. The region between Jacobs Lake and the North Rim of the Grand Canyon is slightly concave like a bowl, riven with narrow canyons and ridges. The settlers quickly discovered travel was much easier following a drainage like Nail Canyon rather than riding down one ridge and up another.

Just over 25 miles southeast of Pipe Springs, a stream of water gushes down a hillside to fill a pool in a green meadow at the site of an old Forest Service camp. The spring is one of several found along Nail Canyon. This beautiful canyon became the rural route to the north rim of the Grand Canyon. Nail Canyon lies along a north-south alignment. Vertical fractures in the exposed rock layers provide a conduit to the surface for aquifers caught in the deep limestone karst. Each winter the 8,000 foot high plateau is covered with snow, recharging the aquifer.

Big Spring camp, North Rim

Big Spring

Warm Springs Canyon, with a thermal spring, intersects the north end of Nail Canyon. Moving south along Nail Canyon, a line of springs emerges from the sandstone walls: Oak Spring, Tilton and Moquitch followed by Mangum, Mourning Dove and Big Spring. At the tail end, Castle and Riggs Springs emerge below Big Spring. All of these flow with water that entered the aquifer in the central region of the Kaibab Plateau.

Big Springs is a gushet emerging from a fracture in the rock on the canyon wall. The Paiute consider the spring to be sacred and it is my understanding that only the men of the tribe are allowed to approach the spring. Women are not allowed to touch the water. This does not deter the tourists that enjoy the grounds of the Forest Service camp, built in 1934. A cluster of small cabins and a cookhouse sit at the north end of the grounds while the southern end is an active Forest Service work site. A Fire Crew lives at the site during the warmer months and can often be seen training when not actively fighting a wild fire. The spring flows into a large pond near the cabins.

In 1871 Levi Stewart, a Bishop in the Church of the Latter Day Saints, moved south from Kanab to establish a ranch and sawmill at Big Springs. His brother-in-law and adult sons followed, homesteading in Demotte Park. Twenty years later, the federal government would begin to set aside land for forest reserves, including the land of some of the homesteaders.

By 1880, each of the Stewart men were called away on missions for the Latter Day Saints and the partnership was dissolved. The ranches sold along with the rights to the springs. Over the next decade, a group in Orderville and later the VT Ranch would begin to run cattle on the Kaibab Plateau.

Harold Bowman and his wife, Nina, lived in Kanab. Like the Stewarts, he enjoyed hunting north of the Canyon and providing meat for his family. However, he longed to go into business for himself. Now he saw a new opportunity in what he would repeatedly call his experiment. The idea was risky, as the traditional route to the Rim passed along Nail Canyon. Bowman convinced his wife that they should establish a roadside stop near Jacob Lake. Loading their truck with supplies, they rattled up the steep slope of the Kaibab Plateau along dirt tracks and set up shop, selling sandwiches, homemade rootbeer and gasoline to loggers, hunters and tourists out of the back of their truck.

Car camping was becoming popular as people began to explore further from home. The first trip by automobile came in 1913 with road construction necessary in some locations along the route. Seven years later, President Woodrow Wilson signed legislation creating the Grand Canyon National Park.

The Bowmans built a small cabin in 1924, selling homemade rootbeer and native crafts to tourists. Nina Bowman and her brother ran the business while Harold cared for business interests in Kanab. With the increase in visitation over the next five years, a new road was to be built to ease travel to the North Rim of the canyon. For years, visitors had been driving down Nail Canyon, crossing over to Demotte Park before turning south toward the Rim.

Bowman saw another opportunity, one that might pass him by. The proposed route for the new road would climb the flanks of the Kaibab Plateau to arrive at the bottom of the hill below Jacob Lake. State engineers then chose a route that turned south across the plateau to Demotte Park. Bowman wanted the road to arrive at his lodge at the top of the hill where he would sell gasoline, water and meals to tourists en route to the Park. Now it seemed this new road would pass him by.

Bowman had a good relationship with the road-building crew due to his years in road construction north of Kanab. It seems one weekend, the crew left the road-building machinery unattended with full tanks of gas and the keys in the ignition! Bowman went to work and over the next two days, carving out a new road that passed directly by the lodge before turning south toward the Rim.

When the crews returned, the work was done. There seemed little point in carving out the road as originally intended. In time, the Bowman and Rich families would carve a road west from Jacob's Lake toward House Rock Valley and the new bridge built over the Colorado River in 1929. As Harold Bowman foresaw, millions of visitors would follow his roads across the Kaibab Plateau.

At first, the visitors camped around the lodge that had grown out of their first cabin. By 1932, John Rich, Harold's son-in-law, and the Bowman-Rich family began building small cabins that would grant visitors more than canvas tents over their heads. Today, the enterprise encompasses the lodge, a number of cabins and hotel rooms, along with a campground. My favorite time at Jacob Lake comes in the cooler months when the fireplace is roaring and summer crowds have faded away. A quiet settles over the Plateau. Those few passing through, swing a leg over a stool at the lunch counter and order a juicy burger.

This is all great except for the absence of water. The Plateau does not contain running streams and sizeable lakes from which to draw drinking water. Early on the Bowman and Rich families recognized the lack of water as inhibiting the growth of their enterprise.

Warm Spring, west of Jacob Lake, is aptly named for a small thermal spring emerging from the canyon wall. To supplement their water collection system, the family began transporting the water from the spring to the lodge. As the demand for water increased, they began transporting from Mangum spring in Nail Canyon as well.

Steve Rich, the grandson of Harold Bowman, recalls that he and his brother John

Warm Springs Canyon Reservoir, water for Jacob Lake Inn

were put to work one summer at Mangum Spring. Steve and his uncle, George, were to install a pipe from the spring down to a terminal and his brother, John, was to build the terminal. A truck would transport the water from the terminal to a 250,000 gallon reservoir at Warm Springs. The Rich family had previously installed a pipeline from Warm Springs up to the lodge. The truck makes four trips a day, hauling a daily total of 28,000 gallons between reservoir and lodge.

At first they also hauled a load from Big Springs, supplementing the supply from Mangum and Warm Springs. This arrangement ended when the state determined that their collection system at Big Springs did not meet health standards. At one point a roof collection system was also installed at the lodge to supplement what was pumped from the springs.

When John Rich, Steve's brother passed away in 2019, he had been working to obtain grants to run a pipeline from Mangum to Warm Springs to save the cost of hauling water. That plan remains stalled until a family member might choose to see the project completed. When visitors enter the restrooms at Jacob Lake, a small sign above the sink reminds them to conserve water as supplies are limited.

As the family prepares to pass the tradition of running the lodge down to the next generation, Melinda, daughter of Steve and Melinda Rich, chose to write about her great grandfather's experiment at Jacob Lake. She chose to use the word *palimsest* to describe how each generation has come to the forests on the Plateau to work in the family enterprise and left their own legacy on the Inn. A palimsest is a parchment or skin once used for writing a document. Such material was expensive and rare. To gain maximum use, when a palimsest had served its purpose, the surface would be scraped clean, turned 90 degrees and written across once again. After it was scraped, Melinda notes that traces of the original writing remained and could still be read. Some of the parchments were used several times, each layer still visible to the scribe.

Over the years the site and buildings at Jacob Lake have been used and refashioned multiple times to serve new purpose just as a palimsest was used repeatedly centuries ago. In the summer of 2020, with the outbreak of the Covid virus, the room that was once her grandmother's livingroom was transformed from the employees' break room to a station for lodgers to pick up food orders.

The history of her family over four generations is written across Jacob Lake Inn, a crossroads for a pioneer people. The springs of Nail Canyon have played a silent but vital role in that history.

We could say that this is true of many of the towns in Arizona. Certainly Flagstaff and Tucson gives glimpses in their architecture and in their festivals celebrating the generations who have come and gone. The springs remain and yet, they are altered as well. Many bear the stories of those who have come before and left traces of their lives imprinted on the land around the springs.

Like Jacob Lake and Warm Spring, Big Spring has evolved from a role as the headquarters of a ranch to a Forest Service Camp. The water that gushes from the spring supports the Forest Service Camp and maintains a small grove of trees planted as part of a Forestry Study.

Just beyond Big Springs is Castle spring. Recently a number of Hopi young people and elders came to the massive rock face that overhangs an alcove under which a stream of water trickles from a crack in the cliff.

Cattle were drawn to the spring to quench their thirst. Their hooves tore up the soft ground. The remnants of ranching operations littered the meadow bordering the sandstone ridge. In a sense, the same concept that Melinda Rich discussed in her thesis is shown by the creosote and the discarded timbers, a history written across stone and meadow.

The Hopi, working with Northern Arizona University and the Forest Service arrived to restore Castle Spring. The spring is revered by the Paiute, the Ute, the Hopi and the Navajo. This is a beautiful site, with the upward sweep of white Coconino sandstone looming over the green of willows and pine. The meadow, lush and verdant from the winter storms, is rimmed with aspen and pine.

The discard of the old corrals and loading chute, along with trash and invasive species lay tangled with brush and aspen. The group, including Hopi youth and elders, along with Forest Service personnel, began to remove much of the old timber and the trash. They pulled the invasive species and cut back the native vegetation crowding the spring.

The water emerges from a deep cleft in the rock face and along fractures in the rock overhead. The Hopi built a pool with native rock. A channel allows overflow to trickle along a pipe to a wooden trough where wildlife can quench their thirst. Some of the water still leaks across the ground and betrays the footprints of those who come to visit the spring. A sturdy fence helps to keep cattle out of the pool and overhang. Visitors step through a narrow gap in the fence.

A sign requests that campers place their camps a quarter mile from a spring or reservoir to allow the animals access to the water source. Along the fence, the prints of a deer in the mud speak of animals sidling out of the tree-lined fringe to the water after dark, listening for the tell-tale sound of a predator staking out the spring. The Hopi returned to their mesas and Forest Service personnel to their administrative site, each hoping to cooperate in restoring other springs.

Castle Spring, opposite page

Downstream from Blue Spring on the Little Colorado River.

The Color Blue

Blue Spring is located in the canyon of the Little Colorado River. The surface water flowing along the Little Colorado out of the White Mountains may be clear some months or filled with brown sediment after a good rain. The water emerging from Blue Spring is a light blue. Why the difference?

Salt! Large beds of salt deposits lie under the surface near Holbrook. The Coconino aquifer is recharged along a series of ridges south of Flagstaff. Initially the ground water flows north. As the subsurface flows move beyond Holbrook, the water turns toward the northwest.

Water passing through the salt deposits picks up dissolved sediments that give the water a blue tint. This presents us with a new perspective on the water that flows blue around our state.

Blue Spring is a major point of discharge for the Coconino aquifer. The water from Blue spring enters the deep green waters of the Colorado River, swirling as runoff from an artist's palette.

Remnant of an Ancient Sea

For centuries, water and snow melt slid across the grainy sandstone of Black Mesa and the Moencopi Plateau.* In turn, for centuries the Hopi people have relied on the springs that emerged along the edge of the plateau to pool in washes like Moencopi and Pasture Canyon. Nearly 400 springs rise from aquifers across Hopi ancestral lands and the Navajo Nation.

To the Hopi people, the water that emerges is more than a cool drink or sustenance for their crops and livestock. They believe the water carries the spirits that sustain them. Caught in the flow of hydrogen and oxygen molecules in each drop is life itself. The word *Moencopi* is translated as 'flowing water.' The village is located on the flanks of the Moencopi Plateau near Tuba City. The homes resemble the traditional architecture of the pueblos, once the home of the pueblo people across the northern reaches of Arizona and New Mexico.

Why would the Hopi have chosen to build one of their villages, particularly one devoted to farming, within this broad wash? Many of their traditional villages were built atop the mesas to the east where they could be defended from raiding parties of other tribes. The answer lies in the water that leaks from walls of the cliffs that tower over the wash as well as runoff during the seasons of precipitation.

Look at region surrounding Moencopi on a satellite map. Two slender lines of deep green crease the mesa in a sea of pale sandstone. These streaks of green are Moencopi Wash and Pasture Canyon.

For those driving north along US89A, the landscape may seem like a giant sandbox with sandstone ridges and waves molded from ancient grit. High on the cliffs, isolated pinyon pine and juniper spring from the fractured rock as an exclamation point to the red hues of sandstone. This scarified land would hardly seem to have a vast aquifer hidden under the rock. Yet, not just one but several aquifers have formed within the rock layers, making their presence known by the tiny seeps that nourish hints of green along the sandstone ridges.

The Dakota and Navajo formations contain the primary aquifers on the western half of these native lands. Further east toward the state line with New Mexico, the Bidahochi and Toreva aquifers overlie the Navajo aquifer. Under

---

* Moencopi may also be spelled Moenkopi. The Hopi call the village, Munqapi.

Moencopi Wash and the village of Moencopi

these three aquifers lies the Coconino aquifer. Some hydrogeologists suggest that these smaller aquifers may feed the deeper Coconino aquifer.

The aquifer found in Navajo sandstone is the key source of water to both the Hopi and the Navajo. At the northern edge the layers of Navajo sandstone lie a thousand feet thick, top to bottom, but peter out on the southern edge to just 200 feet. Lower Moencopi sits within Moencopi Wash, along the western edge of the Navajo aquifer. The homes overlook the canyon floor carpeted with fields of corn.

Pasture Canyon flows south into Moencopi Wash but unlike the larger wash, seems to be left to natural vegetation. In the late 1800s, LDS settlers constructed a dam deep within Pasture Wash to retain both seasonal runoff and the discharge from the springs. Over the years the dam has been repeatedly built higher to contain more water used for irrigation.

Some anthropologists believe Moencopi was first established as a farming community for those living in Oraibi on Third Mesa. The distance between the two villages is about 45 miles cross-country. Unlike Moencopi, Oraibi was built on top of the mesa. Oraibi Wash runs for miles to deposit sediment on the high plains north of Flagstaff. The vertical walls of the wash stand high overhead - an example of how the force of water can alter the natural streambed. There is little to slow the flow of water as it rushes off the mesa and in that flow, the water cuts vertical walls along the watercourse. The force of the water is not hospitable to a Hopi farmer. However, washes feeding into Oraibi Wash often have corn fields where the flooding may not be as strong.

Historically, the Hopi placed their fields in the mouth of the canyons that retained top soil swept down from the mesas. Flooding saturated the soil. The water remained in the sediment layers, held by a subsurface impervious layer. The Pima practiced the same techniques in the washes feeding the Gila River. Not only did the water flow across the surface but under the surface as well, leaving the sandy soil moist at depth.

    Many of the Hopi springs traditionally did not produce a large volume of water. The water was collected in large ollas or pots and used for cooking and bathing rather than gardening. Wepo Spring on First Mesa once produced around 30 gallons a minute and this was channeled to some gardens as was the water from some of the springs near the ancient village of Awat'ovi before it was destroyed. *

    Corn is a staple for both Hopi and Navajo. Traditionally, a farmer would push his stick deep into the alluvial deposits, placing the kernals of corn 10 to 18 inches below the surface. Each deposit was placed several feet apart. And then the farmer waited, his timing based on the seasons. Today, Hopi farmers use tractors but they still relie on the seasonal precipitation.

    Hopi lands receive two seasons of precipitation: the first in the winter with snowmelt, the second with the summer rains. As temperatures warm in the spring, runoff floods the arroyos, bringing water to the fields. The kernals take advantage of the moisture that recedes below the surface. While the dirt at the surface may appear dry, a foot deep the moisture is not wicked up to the surface to evaporate. This moisture nourishes the kernal as it sprouts and begins to grow. In mid-July, the summer rains arrive and allow the corn to mature.

Hopi corn field

    Along with the corn, the Hopi historically grew winter squash and beans in seasonal gardens. A small amount of cotton was also raised. When the Spanish arrived, tomatoes, peppers and melons were introduced along with fruit trees bearing apples, peaches and apricots. For centuries, the springs nourished the pueblo people.

    This cycle is at the heart of Hopi beliefs. The Hopi see water underneath the earth's surface as a living, breathing world called Patuwaqatsi, meaning 'water life.' They believe that their ancestors once lived peaceably in a third world where all

---

* Roads in the Sky: The Hopi Indians in a Century of Change, Richard O. Clemmer, Westview Press, 1995

was in balance. Each person was responsible for their own thoughts and actions, working for the good of the community.

In Hopi belief, this third world was destroyed as immorality became prevalent. As the third world began to flood, Maasaw, the creator, led the people along a cane reed to a hole in the sky where they emerged into the fourth world. For some clans, the point of emergence was Sipapuni. The Hopi people believe that when they die they return to the third world, becoming one of the Cloud People. As the season of the Kachinas arrives, ceremonies are performed in the villages to draw the Cloud people back to the mesas. The Cloud People draw moisture to the roots of the corn and to the squash and beans in their gardens. As the Cloud People arrive, they shed rain as blessings to their descendants and cause the corn to grow that will sustain the Hopi. *

Hopi Chairman Vernon Masayesva summed up Hopi belief, *"All is born of water . . . All is sustained by water."*

> **Many Native tribes regard springs as:**
>
> * Their point of origin.
> * A site for cultural ceremonies.
> * A site along traditional routes to rest and trade.
> * A classroom to train children and teenagers.
> * Water for gardens and fields.
> * A site to find traditional herbs.
> ~ Springs Stewardship Institute

Surface well in Moencopi Wash, mid summer.

This tradition varies with the clans but each unique version holds the same elements of destruction and salvation. Their beliefs are the essence of their survival. Each new development produced by society is weighed and discussed to determine whether it is line with their beliefs or contrary to the heritage of the Cloud people. As a result, the clans have taken different routes over the last two hundred years, some choosing a traditional route, others are described as progressive.

With the increasing population on Hopi lands, townsites have changed and roads have been paved. The springs faced challenges from sedimentation, poor drainage, and contamination from outhouses. Each of these concerns has been addressed. In some communities, outhouses have been replaced with modern

* Paahu and Hopi Tradition, Kristian Diaz, 2011.

plumbing. Natural Channel Design, a company based in Flagstaff, has improved drainage and design around other springs in order to provide a more natural flow.

Like the Hopi, the Navajo relied on the springs for water, though their spiritual beliefs are not bound to the springs. As the Navajo began to settle into a lifestyle that relied less on raiding and more on the planting of corn, they took up the practice of raising sheep. Many of the sheep herders depend on the springs for water for their herds. In the 1800s, settlers from the Latter-Day Saints entered the Hopi communities and dug wells tapping the Dakota aquifer. Tribal wells now reach the Navajo aquifer. The well at Moencopi is 700 feet deep with a casing down the first 300 feet.

The central region of the Navajo Nation does not have the quantity of springs found along the western and eastern edges of the Navajo aquifer. Much of the Navajo aquifer in the central region is confined or under pressure from the rock layers above. According to studies done by the United States Geological Survey, the Navajo aquifer is believed to recharge in the northern and central region, receiving 2,600 acre feet or more of water each year. The aquifer discharges along the western and eastern borders.

Further east toward the border with New Mexico, the Bidahochi and Toreva aquifer overlay the Navajo aquifer. The Toreva aquifer is found in shallow bands of sandstone while the Bidahochi is found in pockets of sandstone near the surface that remain from a sandstone layer that once covered this region. Much of the Bidahochi formation has been eroded and is now visible in a limited number of locations. Many of the springs the Navajo sheep herders first relied on were supplied by water ascending from the Bidahochi formation. The earliest wells in the eastern half of the Navajo Nation also drew from the Bidahochi aquifer. Today many of the springs have ceased to flow as the Bidahochi is effected by years of drought.

While the Navajo Nation and the Hopi obtain water from wells drilled into the Navajo aquifer that is clear and good in taste, another layer of rock makes the task of finding water in these dry lands more challenging. Jason Johns, Director for the Navajo Department of Water Resources, describes this formation as mudstone or siltstone.

Think of wading into a shallow backwater of a creek. As

you approach, the water looks clear with every speck on the bottom easily seen. But, dip a toe into the pool lightly touching the bottom and a cloud of silt rises to obscure everything. This is the birthplace of mudstone. Silt once flowed from surrounding hills into a vast area of shallow water. As the silt hardened, a fine-grain rock formed that retains very little water.

The thick bands of mudstone inhibit the task of bringing water to the Navajo people. When a thin trickle of muddy, poor tasting water rises to the surface, the drill crew knows they have hit mudstone rather than the the Navajo aquifer.

Locating a good aquifer is just one problem for the Navajo Nation. In the 19th and 20th centuries, many homes and industries were heated with coal. If the Navajo Nation had a resource, it was coal. At one time 21% of the U.S. bituminous coal reserves were located on the Navajo Nation. Black Mesa, with rich coal beds caught the attention of an international mining company.

Energy companies wishing to do exploratory drilling on Black Mesa found that they would be required to form an agreement with each village before they could begin operating on Hopi land. The Bureau of Indian Affairs also did not have a focal point in talking with the Hopi tribe. Commissioners encouraged the tribe to select a representative from each village to form a council with a Chairman as was found with many of the other tribes. This would be the foundation in the years that followed for conflict between those who followed the tradition and those who wished to move forward toward assimilation into the white culture.

The energy companies now had a council for their negotiations. The mineral leasing began with oil wells that proved to be dry. As those seeking oil reserves moved onto other regions, the bed of coal became the primary focus.

In 1964, the directors of Peabody Energy entered negotiations with both the Navajo and Hopi to pump water from the Navajo aquifer. The water would carry coal slurry along a pipeline between the Black Mesa Mine and the Mohave Generating Station on the Colorado River. At the time the Navajo and Hopi did not know that one of their negotiators, John Boyden, was on the Board of Directors for Peabody.

The Navajo Nation signed an agreement with Peabody in 1964 allowing the company to pump three million gallons of water from the Navajo aquifer each day. Two years later in 1966, despite protests from the traditional clans, Peabody signed an agreement with the Hopi Council for their water rights to pump water from the Navajo aquifer. Undoubtably, the Council believed the royalties and the jobs that would be created would be beneficial to their people. There is little industry on native lands. The royalties the Hopi received were considerably less than that received by the Navajos.

There were some irregularities within the agreement. The Hopi Constitution, drawn up when the Council formed, did not give the Council the authority to approve leases on the land in accordance with the traditional means of governance for the Hopi. John Boyden was employed as Chief Council for the Hopi tribe yet continued to sit on the Board of Directors for Peabody for a period of time. The land that Peabody intended to strip mine had been declared a roadless and scenic are by the Department of the Interior. And then, there was the issue of selling the water that the Hopi regarded as sacred.

Vernon Masayesva, former Hopi chairman and resident of the traditional village of Hotevilla, argued, *"The mining of water violates our beliefs. When you sell something sacred, it doesn't sit right. It sits on your conscience."*

Years later, activists would say that the Navajo and Hopi people got a raw deal out of these agreements. The agreement was very good for Peabody. The energy giant began paying $1.67 for each acre foot of water when the going rate was between $30 to $40 an acre foot. This water was high quality suitable for municipal drinking water. *

The Navajo aquifer was thought to store 180 million acre feet of water. Peabody began pumping three million gallons of water from the aquifer every day from 1966 to 2005, when they were forced to discontinue using the aquifer. Using these numbers, without consideration for any shutdowns that may have occurred in the course of a year, the mine pulled over 100 million gallons of water from the aquifer which equates to 3,240 acre feet of water. This was an unsustainable withdrawal in a land that receives only 12 to 18 inches of precipitation each year. *

Peabody argued that the Navajo aquifer could sustain these large withdrawals. However, by 1969, the water level in wells near the Black Mesa mine had dropped seven feet. In the 1970's Navajo sheepherders and the Hopi people began to notice the springs were diminishing but their cries went unanswered. Activists brought their plea to public forums.

Prior to 1969, average withdrawal was around 300 acre feet across both reservations. By 1971 the withdrawal had surged to 4,200 feet. By the late 1990's, the Navajo aquifer was being stripped of water faster than it could recover. With the drought that has plagued the southwest for over twenty years, many of the springs simply disappeared.

Lawsuits filed by Hopi traditionalists in 1964 and again in 1971, failed to overturn the agreements. In 1980, the Hopi Tribe commissioned an independent environmental study. The result indicated that water was being pumped from above the 2,000 level where the tribes received it drinking water. The study also showed that the water table had dropped from 10 feet to as much as 30 feet depending on the location.

The time came for Peabody to develop a new section of the coal reserves that had not been touched. Before the company could build a road into the

* Roads in the Sky: The Hopi Indians in a Century of Change, Richard O. Clemmer, Westview Press, 1995
* Hopi has received only eight inches of precipitation the last few years, akin to a desert climate.

section, permission had to be obtained from the Hopies. The Hopi Council used the permit as a means to insist on a new Environmental Impact Statement. This time, the study showed the effects of the withdrawal of vast amounts of water. The mine had become an eyesore and Peabody had failed to restore much of the area previously mined in acccord with the original agreement. The ecosystem had been irreversibly damaged and sacred sites violated. Both the Navajo and Hopi Councils refused to grant access to the new site.

Along with the Environmental Impact Statement, the 10 year recertification for the Mohave Generating Station on the Colorado River came due. Part of the recertification was the renewal of the agreement that gave Peabody the right to pump water from the Navajo Aquifer. The Hopis were no longer willing to sell their birthright. Without water or access to their next site, Peabody Energy was forced to stop pumping water from the aquifer. *

This time Peabody filed suit against the tribes and the judge found that the tribes had not received adequate representation nor had their objections been adequately considered when the agreement was first signed. The mine remained closed and new lawsuits were filed. Today, due to the ongoing legal action, officials from the Hopi tribe would not talk to me about the springs or aquifers. Much of the information regarding the dispute between Peabody and the tribes is found online.

In 2015, total discharge from the springs studied, ranged from 360 to 1,100 gallons a minute. A study by the Arizona Department of Water Resources found that of 221 springs surveyed on Hopi lands, an effort had been made to modify or improve the outlet with 83 of the springs. Many of the springs have been effected by sedimenatation or the water channel has been damaged.

Fifteen years after the shutdown, a few isolated wells have shown an improvement, but overall there is no indication that the aquifer is being restored to its former levels. The population around Tuba City has increased, placing a further strain on the western edge of the Navajo aquifer.

In 1964, water use was around 100 acre feet a year in the more populated areas of the western Navajo Nation. By 1983, water usage had increased to 120 acre feet annually in Tuba City and 45 acre feet in Kayenta. Like much of the state, the tribes recycle their effluent. No one is certain as to how the aquifer will respond in the years ahead now that the pumping has ended and the drought continues.

There is one other threat to the springs on the Navajo and Hopi lands. During the 1950's the United States and the Soviet Union were in a stand-off. Each side was convinced that the other would attempt domination through the use of nuclear weapons. Uranium and plutonium are the fuels for nuclear weapons.

* Ibid

The walls of Moencopi Wash reveal the aquifer hidden in the sandstone. Notice the vegetation at the foot of the sheer cliff where water has leaked from fractures, giving life to windblown seeds that take root above State Route 264.

Northern Arizona, particularly the Grand Canyon and the Navajo Nation, hold uranium deposits. Today, abandoned uranium mines dot reservation lands. Permits have been requested to open or expand uranium mines on land bordering the Grand Canyon. One report to the Coconino Plateau Advisory Meeting noted that both the Canyon mine and the Orphan mine are located 1,000 feet above the aquifer with no leakage expected to pass down to the groundwater. Generally, uranium deposits are stable as long as they remain undisturbed.

One site of great concern to the Havasupai Tribe is the Canyon Mine and a request for a permit to mine a breccia pipe with uranium deposits at 1,000 feet below the surface. Would the mine shaft intersect a perched aquifer thought to lay around 900 feet below the surface? Much deeper than the proposed shaft is the Muav aquifer at 2,560 feet. Does the perched aquifer feed the Muav aquifer?

The Havasupai depend on the springs within their canyon walls. The Arizona Department of Environmental Quality has asked the owners of Canyon Mine to apply for an individual water permit which with the intention to monitor the region's groundwater.

Mining activities leave behind waste products which may become a threat to the springs. The dirt around the mine sites is radioactive. Ponds of water containing radioactive sludge may leak into the ground. At one time radioactive tailings were discarded near Tuba City. The tailings are now part of a slow drift creeping toward one of the Hopi springs. The federal government continues to wrangle with the tribes over who bears the responsibility to clean up the tailings. The disagreement is unlikely to be resolved soon.

Of Apple Trees and Leopard Frogs

The origin of the Huachuca Mountains in southern Arizona began in volcanic activity that left mineral-rich deposits of rhyolite and basalt. The range is part of the Madrean Archipelgo and is a refuge for the high country species in the low country of southern Arizona. While winter temperatures may be moderate, Miller Peak with an elevation just over 9,000 feet may receive snow from winter storms. In July and August summer rains sweep up from the Gulf of California to drench the rock cliffs and deep pine glades. The sky-sent precipitation in both seasons each contribute to the perched aquifers that lie within these peaks. At the base of the range, are deeper aquifers caught in the grit and rock that has eroded from the high slopes.

As with any rock formation born of volcanic activity a number of faults run through the range. These faults allow the water held in the aquifers to rise to the surface. Springs found in Miller and Carr Canyons on the eastern exposure of the range became the lifeline of Tombstone and later the grounds for extensive legal action as the region developed.

One of the most notable springs on of the eastern side of the Huachucas is Bathtub spring, elevation 8,420 feet. True to its name, a porcelain bathtub contains water trickling from the hillside spring. The history of the bathtub originates with the sons of a local rancher who developed a reputation for taking on odd challenges such as dragging an old bathtub up the steep slopes of the Huachucas. Hikers along the Arizona trail frequently stop to take photos. The quality of the water mixed with the algae growing in the tub make it unpalatable.

A second spring with a colorful reputation can be found in an arroyo on the lower end of Carr Canyon that was home to an illegal still during the years of Prohibition. Having heard the story from a long-time Bisbee resident, I have never been able to learn anything more of the site or the still.

In the mid 1800s, prospectors labored across the mountain ranges of southern Arizona, seeking signs of mineralization. Several old mine shafts can be found on the slopes of the Huachucas that once produced silver and copper ore.

Carr Spring is located above the Reef Townsite Mine, overlooking the town of Sierra Vista below. Historically, the spring supplied water to both a sawmill and the Reef Mine. After the mine closed, the Forest Service built a campground on the site. A pipe once brought water from the spring to a small campground where hikers once filled their water bottles from the pipe. In recent years the spring began to run dry.

One concern in drinking from any spring is the presence of harmful bacteria. The water may look clear and clean but what is invisible to the human eye? In the case of Carr Canyon, a ranger would regularly arrive to dump an appropriate amount of chlorine into the water to kill whatever bacteria might have emerged from the spring. Testing was done periodically but fell below the standard expected with our urban water systems.

There are two springs that we will consider in the Huachucas. One supported a cluster of mining sites, the other would be seldom noticed by all but hunters and the activity along the border with Mexico in recent years.

Ramsey Canyon

As with many canyons in the Madrean sky islands, Ramsey is a unique ecological environment. The springs of Ramsey Canyon are a large part of making the canyon so attractive to man and the diverse wildlife. With the presence of running water, Ramsey offers a refuge to species that could not survive in the desert. Over 170 species of birds, including the Scarlet Trogen live in the canyon. Some, like Rivoli's and Anna's hummingbirds, migrate north to Arizona during the warm summer months, returning to Mexico each fall.

Maples and sycamore along with columbine line the moist banks of the creek. Cactus and agave appear among the water loving species. The stream trickles over large granite boulders, rushing into a maelstrom during snow melt in the spring.

Ramsey Canyon spring

Over the years I've enjoyed visiting the Ramsey Canyon Preserve but in researching the springs, I saw the canyon in a new light. As we started walking up the canyon, I was visually searching the banks of the stream for some evidence of a spring flowing from the hillside. Just steps from the Visitors Center was a patch of scouring reeds, one of the signatures of a health spring. The reeds absorb and clean impurities that may flow with the water coming out of the spring. I had never noticed the abundance of this endemic species but now the reeds seemed to be every few feet. Looking closer, I could see water seeping from fractured rock above the water line.

Scouring reeds

A short distance up the canyon from the Visitors Center is a cement spring box embedded in the hillside. We found the box open to the sky, with vertical sides and an open front. The back was set against a large fractured rock. Plastic sheeting served as a roof, keeping most of the leaves of the arboreal canopy from fouling the spring's outlet. The box contained several inches of water. At one time, a pipe channeled the water to the orchard and homes below. The size of the spring box indicates this was a perennial spring that once provided a good amount of water.

The canyon itself is a series of eroded fault lines with the roots of mature sycamores and maples creeping deep into the ruptured rock. The bed of dried leaves disguises the irregular surface around the spring, making it easy to misstep into the overflow and mud several inches deep.

The water in this lower spring may come from an aquifer in the Permian limestone formation just north of the canyon. The ridge above the spring where the Hamburg mine is located is of igneous origin with granite and basalt. Beneath the igneous layer may be sedimentary layers while the plains below hold alluvial deposits that contribute to the San Pedro River.

We continued to hike beyond the cabins and pools contained within the Nature Conservancy, following a trail toward the Hamburg Mine. The Nature Conservancy trail crosses the stream and turns back to the Visitors Center, while the trail to the Hamburg Mine climbs a steep ridge through a series of switchbacks. A docent had directed us further up the canyon to a second spring high on a hillside above the Preserve. A grassy bank gave us a clue that there was more to this pocket than a just a rocky knoll.

Stream flowing through Ramsey Canyon

> Throughout the streambed, the rock weeps, bringing tears to the mountain canyon.

Stepping off the trail, we discovered a small round pool at the base of an Arizona sycamore. Water skater bugs flexed across the still surface. Leaning over the dark surface, we could catch the reflection of our trail-worn appearance as if peering into a darkened mirror. No current appeared to direct the water down the hillside, but a few feet away, a dark mire pulled at my boots. The pool, only a few inches deep, is fed by a perched aquifer with alluvial fill trapped in a pocket on the slopes of a high peak. A rock lip prevents the alluvium from descending down the slope. The alluvium absorbs the moisture that falls on the peak, creating the perched aquifer.

For those who have read the stories of C.S. Lewis, the pool reminded me of The Magician's Nephew. I wondered in my imagination, if I jump feet first into the pool, would I be sucked away to another world? My partner sprawled on the grass as I snapped images from one angle, then another. We didn't jump. As temperatures warm in the summer months, I suspect the spring would slowly fade as the mining town had a century before.

In the 1870's, prospectors found ore deposits in upper Ramsey Canyon near the junction of Pat Scott Canyon and Wisconsin Canyon. The discovery brought civilization into the canyon along with the development of of the Hamburg Mine.

The site of a dance pavilion under the sycamore trees.

    In 1900, a mining company filed claims for what would became the Hamburg mine, named for Superintendent Henry Hamburg. Around 150 men were employed at the Hamburg Mine. Records indicate the mine had a level entrance leading to a 200 foot tunnel with pits and several small drifts of discarded material.

    A small town was nestled two miles from the entrance of the canyon with boarding houses, a saloon and a general store for the miners. A sawmill was installed and men began cutting beams to stabilize the mine shafts. The sawmill only remained for two years, and like the mine, used the water from the springs high in the hills above the canyon. The mine operated from 1900 to 1950 with up to 100 tons of ore shipped down the canyon to the railhead near Hereford on the San Pedro River.

    The first man to homestead in Ramsey Canyon was Gordon Ramsey. He built a road that followed the steep terrain up to the Hamburg Mine. He moved his family into the canyon in 1879 even as the miners were blasting the rock into mineral-laden ore. In 1902, John James brought his family to the canyon and built a small cabin that still stands creekside. The James family found their homesite received only a few hours of sunlight and the moist climate left their cabin cold even during the day. Due to the short hours of sunlight, they struggled to make the homestead a success. By 1911, the James abandoned their first cabin and build a larger home downstream on the opposite bank where sunlight warmed the rocks in the afternoon.

A year earlier in 1910, William Berner brought new interest to the canyon, building some small cabins and advertizing for tourists who wished to escape the warm summer temperatures in Tucson. To provide entertainment, he added a dance hall with a pavilion that wrapped around one of the huge sycamores on the canyon floor. While a German orchestra from Bisbee played, patrons enjoyed beer from a local distillery.

He built large wooden tubs and reportedly there is a photo in state archives that shows the visitors soaking in the cool water during a warm afternoon. His primary occupation, however, was planting and nurturing large apple orchards in the lower end of the canyon. With the moderate climate and water seeming to leak through every rock crevice, the apple trees flourished and Berner began shipping apples to Tucson and Phoenix.

Not to be outdone, many of the early settlers began planting apple trees to supplement their garden vegetables. By the 1970s, many of the apple trees had aged beyond a bountiful production. The land in the upper canyon had been purchased by Dr. Nelson Bledsoe, a physician who practiced in Tucson and Sierra Vista for six decades. He loved the canyon and built a home as a retreat where he lived in his retirement. He wished to see the canyon protected and oversaw the acquisition of his property by the Nature Conservancy.

The Nature Conservancy did not view the canyon as a place for road-worn visitors to run unchecked along the stream. The goal of the Conservancy is to return land to a healthy natural state within reasonable expectation. They began by removing many of the old structures along with the apple trees that crowded the canyon floor. The stream was restructured to a more natural flow, with water dropping over large granite boulders and slaloming through scouring reeds and underbrush beneath mature cottonwoods.

The canyon is home to the endangered Chiricahua leopard frogs as well as the hummingbirds, black bear, white-tail deer, coatimundi and many of the creatures that inhabit the wild country of Arizona. These residents will not pop out in front of a visitor's camera lens, but wait for the evening shadows to cloak the creek before moving down to the water.

As part of the restoration, the Conservancy built large ponds high on its property to encourage the leopard frogs to re-establish their population. When we last hiked the canyon, the pools looked raw, as if flooding had swept through, destroying some of the previous work. Visitors can walk along one side of the ponds but rarely catch a glimpse of this species as they burrow into the mud.

During the early summer the stream may shrink to small pools with only a trickle of water tracing the stream course. As the humidity increases in late June, windows are flung open to reduce the oppressive atmosphere. Residents daily check the forecast, awaiting the arrival of the summer rains. When they arrive in early July, the creek fills again, spilling and dancing over the rocks. Who needs an orchestra and dance pavilion with water music filling the canyon?

Bear Spring

Just as Spanish settlers once moved into New Spain's borderlands, so now brown faces tumble over the international border, seeking a new life with higher wages.

Unlike popular Ramsey Canyon, Bear Spring on the southwestern exposure of the Huachuca Mountains would rarely rate a visit if it were not for the traffic along the border. Bear is a hillside spring a short distance off the Arizona Trail (AT) that crests the Huachuca range. To reach the spring from the AT, hikers would have to scramble down a steep hillside covered with brush. The Huachucas have a reputation for being a rough, steep jumble of rock.

When my husband came of the age to join his father and his father's friends in hunting the elusive Coues Whitetail deer, they would assemble at a camp on the small stream that runs down Bear Canyon. Along with washing dishes and personal hygiene, the trickle of the creek was a pleasure to camp alongside as they told stories through the early evening hours. Before light they would rise sleepy-eyed to begin the long walk up Lone Mountain into a high saddle below Bear Spring. Working as a team, they would push the deer toward a hunter waiting below who filled his family's freezer for the months ahead.

After he moved to northern Arizona, Ken considered returning to the Huachucas to hunt for another season. On a scouting trip, we camped along the stream in Bear Canyon. I knew we were within a half mile of the international border but Ken was only mildly concerned about immigrants who might pass our camp under the cover of darkness.

And pass they did, their canteens clanking on their hips as they walked. In the hills above, the coyotes sang. Clank, clank. Gunshots rang out from the mine on the hillside above us as a caretaker objected to the presence of the immigrants. The coyotes stopped singing. Soon another band of immigrants came along. Clank, clank. I was sure they could see the flicker of our lantern and hoped they would not come into our camp.

In the morning, we climbed a ridge, stepping around a long line of volcanic rock that seemed like a primitive wall left by an ancient tribe. Well above the road, in a pocket tucked out of sight lay a trail of trash: Discarded backpacks, electrolyte bottles, a blanket, papers softly waving in the breeze. All of it left by the those who cross the border illegally and climb through the mountains because they have been told that they will find work in the city just over the hill.

What would bring the immigrants to cross at such an isolated stretch of the border? Why would they choose to climb the steep slopes of a range rising to over 9,000 feet at the summit when there are other regions much easier to cross? There are no trails on the southern slopes, the terrain so rugged that it would be

Pools along Bear Creek

easy to snap an ankle in the darkness shrouding the precipitous climb. The answer in part lies with the water emerging from Bear Spring and the other springs that dot the Huachucas.

The spring has not been diverted, the water left to flow unhindered. The trash on the slope below marks the route to the spring where immigrants can refill their water bottles before pushing north. If not for the immigrants, the only visitors to the spring would be the wildlife or a hiker off the beaten track.

Miles below the outlet, the water passes under a bridge en route to the border. The bridge carries traffic between the Coronado National Monument and Parker Lake. It allows the Border Patrol, ranchers and off-road enthusiasts access to the southern slopes of the Huachucas. The invitation of the clear green pools below the bridge does not go unnoticed. One pool, then another is lined with red rock. These pools are a favorite stop on a warm day. The red rock is an aggregate with a gritty surface studded by well-rounded river rock. This layer speaks of rock that can hold an aquifer deep within the earth. The water from Bear Spring splashes down the steep slope to flow through the pools.

All along the border lie spring that provide water to early tribes as they migrated with the seasons. Today, the pools and Bear Spring have created a route for the trespasser who for whatever reason has chosen to bypass the legal channels, crossing the border under the curtain of darkness. The trash piles are their calling cards.

"We were here. We seek life."

Raising Fish

Arizona was officially recognized as a territory in 1863 as conservationists were beginning to recognize that the wildlife once so abundant was now in decline. In 1881, the Territorial Legislature formed the Arizona Fish Commission to improve and oversee distribution of fish imported from the eastern seaboard. The fish were shipped by rail with stops along the route. At each stop, a portion of the stock was withdrawn to support the fisheries in other states. By the time the train reached Arizona, few fish remained in the tanks to assist our state in increasing our stock of commercially viable fish. Arizona sportsman recognized the need to begin raising home-grown fish for Arizona's lakes and streams.

The Department of State Game Warden was created in 1913. As the state began to grow, sportsmen banded together to keep the management of fish and game animals out of the political arena. In 1929, the Department of Game and Fish was created.

The first hatchery was located on the South Fork of the Colorado River near Eager in 1922. Work crews began building 70 hatching troughs, the rearing ponds and a residence for the manager. The hatchery was not completed until 1924 when negotiations with all interested parties, including the Apache tribe, were resolved. With the first winter setting in, a problem arose. The hatchery was using water from the South Fork of the Little Colorado. When water temperatures remained cooler than expected the manager found the imported stock had died. No fish!

Biologists and hatchery managers recognized that future hatcheries must use water that remained around 55 degrees despite the temperature of the air - in other words, water from Arizona's springs. Several springs were found to offer a sufficient flow. The state began building a new hatchery at Horton Springs, northeast of the town of Payson.

Starting in 1928, the hatchery shipped 750,000 fish to streams in the White Mountains. But in 1932, the foundation for the nursery troughs began to give way. The trough slipped into the creek and was dismantled by the current. The hatchery was never rebuilt.

Sterling Spring Hatchery

Horton Spring

This beautiful spring tumbles down a rocky hillside from fissures near the base of the Mogollon Rim. The water is cold and clear after filtering through 2,000 feet of rock. The trail to Horton Spring is popular with hikers during the warmer months.

One of the problems of relying on water from the springs arose when managers discovered that the flow could vary from year to year, as it did with Indian Gardens near Payson in the 1930s.

In the early years, only trout were raised. Then, Double Spring Hatchery near Mormon Lake and Hunt Hatchery in Papago Park began raising largemouth bass. Hunt Hatchery began raising blue gill and crappie as they tolerated warmer temperatures. By the 1960s, Game and Fish recognized that the warm water fish seemed to reproduce without significant assistance from the State. The bass were multiplying and creating real competition for the trout in some of the northern lakes.

Then, Double Springs was closed due to inadequate flow from the spring and Hunt Hatchery was transferred to the Phoenix Zoo. Pinetop Hatchery became a showpiece for the state from 1932 to 1954 until the springs failed. The hatchery was re-activated in 1997 as the water began to flow again.

Today, the State of Arizona has five hatcheries: Sterling Springs in Oak Creek Canyon, Page Springs near Cottonwood, Tonto Springs east of Payson, Canyon Creek in Forest Lakes, and Silver Creek near Showlow. Two of these hatcheries rely on springs whose use dates back to the earliest days of territorial Arizona. When settlers first came to the northland, the right to Sterling Spring was claimed by the AT&T railroad. As modern engines replaced steam powered engines, the railroad relinquished their claim.

In 1925, sportsmen from the Verde Valley and Flagstaff banded together to build a couple of small rearing ponds below Sterling Spring. Two decades later, in 1948, Game and Fish obtained the rights to the spring and built Sterling Spring Hatchery. When the Pinetop Hatchery was forced to close, more emphasis was placed on raising fish at Sterling Spring. In 1959, the design of the hatchery was changed to a serpentine raceway in an attempt to simulate conditions in the creek. This design was replaced by a standard raceway in the 1970s.

The raceways are well hidden from motorists driving US89A. The canyon is so narrow at this point that only a few hours of sunlight reach the canyon floor. Visitors can gaze up at the canyon walls, towering 1,300 feet over the hatchery. The spring lies in a bend of US89A along the Oak Creek fault. Sterling Spring produces around 280 gallons a minute with the water emerging at a temperature between 48 and 52 degrees.

The spring has been capped and directed into a large underground vault from which a pipe emerges, directing the water into the hatchery. The original pipe was laid in 1949. Walking the length of the pipe I was intrigued to see a seam that spiraled along its length. Most pipe today is created from whole stock rather than rolled.

In 2018, the state, as part of its effort to renovate the hatcheries, removed the cement tanks and began rebuilding modern raceways. The spring water initially flowed through the raceways and returned to Oak Creek. As part of the renovation, a pump was

The spiraling seam along the old pipe at Sterling Spring Hatchery.

installed, recycling water through the tanks when the flow decreases from the spring. Two large vaults were added and drum filters were installed to remove any solid material. A water tower was built with a new aerating system. The valves can release either fresh water or mix recycled water with the fresh water from the spring. A steel awning has been placed over the tanks to provide the shady environment that fish seek in hiding from predators. The business of raising fish is so much more than the early days when spring water poured into a tank and the fish were left to grow to catchable size.

With the tanks completed, a couple of options were considered for the pipeline. The crew could either replace the line or try a new technology which would slide an epoxy-based line inside the old pipe from hatchery to spring. This has become a fairly common practice when the original pipe has not collapsed. In late 2019, the crew arrived and the new line slid neatly into place. No need to replace the older pipe with all the challenges of working in a cramped, steep canyon.

Before the renovation, the Chief of Security, David Fox's large Siberian husky would run along the raceways, springing up on hind legs to place his front paws on the edge. We watched as fish scattered and he ran the length of the raceway. If one should leap into the air, the chief has been known to snatch a quick snack. This is due pay for his important job at the hatchery in keeping an eye on the perimeter for any unwelcome guests.

In the past, otters and raccoons stopped in for an after-hours meal. Fox, the hatchery's manager, found their trails leading under the chain link fence and down to the raceway. He doesn't dislike the otters and raccoons, he just wants them to find their own meals along the creek downstream.

Sterling Springs receives millions of fish eggs early in the year to raise into fingerlings or *sub-catchables*. The eggs are weighed, then placed in a casing that allows the water to circulate continuously as if the egg were in the backwater of a stream. Once the fish hatch, they are transferred to a tank. When the fish reach three inches, they are loaded into truck-borne tanks and driven south to the Page Springs hatchery to be raised to a size where they will be released into the streams and lakes of Arizona.

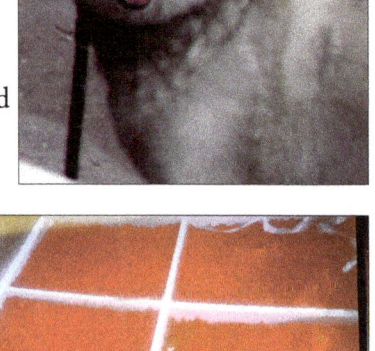

above: Chief of Security
below: Shipment of fish eggs

Of the 280 gallons from the spring, 250 gallons cycle through the hatchery. A second pipeline carries water down to Pine Flat Campground. This water pours from a pipe set high in a spring box along US89A. Cars often line the shoulder of the road as drivers wait their turn to fill large containers with the spring water.

Page Springs Hatchery pond

Two spigots run day and night, the water channeled into Oak Creek.

Oak Creek is primarily fed by springs and runoff from small tributaries. Water levels increase steadily as the stream drops south toward the Verde River. The Trout Farm, just north of Sedona, is located on a spring releasing 1500 gallons a minute. Along with the popular fishing ponds, the spring supplies water to large tanker trucks delivering the water to a bottling plant.

Further downstream at Page Springs, James Page, a local rancher built and maintained four ponds for rearing trout for the residents of the Verde Valley. In 1938, Game and Fish purchased the property from the Arizona Trout Company who had acquired the property from Page. Construction began in 1949 and gave the department 16 concrete raceways, 16 concrete ponds, four circular and four dirt ponds, with a 20-trough hatchery. A cooling tower helped to maintain water temperatures at 68 degrees, the upper level for raising trout.

Today the hatchery is one of the most beautiful in the state, with a large pond and riparian zone. Employees report a variety of amphibians, reptiles, mammals and birds living near the perennial water source. Bubbling Ponds, a second hatchery, is located near Page Springs and raises native Gila trout. The Gila came close to extinction and the program is seeking to restore the native population. After the Wallow Fire, the hatcheries were the key factor in sustaining a breeding stock as debris choked many of the streams in the White Mountains.

The water to support Page Springs hatchery pours out of four springs on the property, together releasing 15 million gallons per day. Once again we look to the massive Mogollon Rim as the source of the water. Twice a year, cycles of precipitation arrive over the northland. The winter months bring snow that percolates down through the rock. Summer rains also bathe the high cliffs with moisture that sweeps north from the Gulf of California. The moisture-laden clouds release torrential rains over the massive uplift. The runoff that does not soak into the thirsty soil gathers in the gullies that riddle central Arizona, flowing in ever larger torrents to the Little Colorado and on to the Colorado River. Along its route the aquifers receive a portion of the runoff.

Visitors exiting their cars at Page Springs are surrounded by the sound of water. To one side, a white-flecked stream of water gushes out of a cave to run along a channel toward the lines of raceways sheltered under a metal awning. Visitors are welcome to walk along the raceways. The fish scatter as visitors approach but when the

One of four springs at Page Spring Hatchery.

intruder sits quietly the fish return. Page Springs is now under threat from a tiny snail. The snails are drawn to the valves that send water into the ponds and eventually grow so numerous that the equipment is clogged. At each of the hatcheries, managers are also vigilant against flavobacterium, a cold water disease effecting rainbow trout. If the bacteria were to enter the hatchery, it could wipe out months of work.

In recent years, vineyards have been planted in the Page Springs valley, lining the hillside with orderly rows of vines. At the Page Springs Cellars, visitors can purchase a goblet of wine with a ploughman's box lunch and proceed to a large deck overlooking the creek. Standing on their deck above the water, I was amazed at how the current had grown in size and force from the small stream we had visited at Sterling Springs Hatchery.

Little Elden Spring

A spring at rest during the winter months remains a quiet refuge for wildlife. On this cold day in February with snow on the ground, Little Elden Spring was not frozen. The spring emerges at the base of a ridge of basalt boulders to form a small pool.

At one time this was a homesite for the Eldens, early settlers in the region around Flagstaff. At one time, it was believed that their son was killed by a muleskinner and buried at the homesite. Descendents of the Elden family recently visited the Pioneer Historical Museum and described the young man's life after he left Flagstaff with his family. Whether there is anyone buried at the site has not been determined.

Hot Water

Morristown, September 1898 – Muttonchop whiskers bristling, a vest strained across his stout chest, the man descended from the rail car. He paused to survey the desert around him. Large boulders weighed down the sandy plain accented with totem saguaro, their arms erect to a brilliant blue sky. He turned to assist a young woman as she gathered her long skirt in one hand. Four children tumbled to the ground behind their mother. They seemed eager to escape the confinement of the rail car, looking for their next adventure.

Already the morning temperatures were warm, so unlike the cool mornings the family had known back east. Two female servants followed the family from the train and nervously looked for snakes that might lurk behind the attendant or the baggage cart. A wiry young man in denim accepted two of the family's cases and carried the luggage to a stagecoach waiting nearby.

Such was the scene at a rail stop along the route between Yuma and Phoenix in the late 1800s. No hotels or fine restaurants stood near the tracks. Just a stagecoach and several shotgun houses along a rail spur. Wealthy clients, including the Vanderbuilts, the Rockefellers and the Carnegies passed through Morristown, transferring their luggage from well-appointed Pullman rail cars to rustic stagecoaches for a twenty-five mile ride through the desert to Castle Hot Springs.

The dirt track led through desert washes, bouncing over rock ledges to arrive at a resort built miles from the nearest town. We can only imagine the shock to a novice making this trip. Reportedly, several US Presidents took the week-long passage by train to arrive at the spur in the middle of the sage and cactus. More than one must have wondered into what he had gotten himself.

Thermal or hot springs have long been in the public narrative. Arizona has a number of hot springs. Most of them are found in the transition zone that spreads in an arc across our state from the southeast border with New Mexico upward to the northeast corner near Boulder Dam. A few of the springs are well known but most are quiet pools in Arizona's back country.

Take a moment to consider the map showing Arizona's thermal springs along with their average temperature. A few, like those around Yuma or in the Grand Canyon, lie outside of the transition zone. You may notice that there are

Opposite page: The pool below Castle Springs, 122 degrees fahrenheit.

several clusters, with the largest being along the southeastern border with New Mexico. Some of these springs are a bare trickle, but others release thousands of gallons a day.

To be considered a thermal spring the water should have an average temperature of 95 degrees fahrenheit or higher. So what process or source heats the water to bathtub temperature? Three sources are considered: heating from volcanic magma, heating from the earth's mantle, and heating from the breakdown of radioactive elements.

Turning to a topographic map of Arizona, we see that much of the central arc across our state contains large mountain ranges. Some of these mountains show volcanic activity as part of their origin. Arizona's volcanoes have been dormant for at least 1,000 years, some dating back to ancient eras. The southeastern corner of our state contains one of the largest volcanic calderas in our country and indeed, there are several clusters of hot springs. We might even suspect the dying embers of the Turkey Creek Caldera as playing a part in heating the springs.

When latent volcanic activity is not evident, scientist look for chemical markers that may indicate another source of heat. The earth's mantle lies from 18 to 35 miles below the earth's crust depending on the location. Heat from the mantle may transfer outward to rocks layers closer to the surface.

A third source could be found in the decay of radioactive elements. One spring outside the transitional zone is capriciously named Radium Hot Spring.

How do scientists determine whether the heating is from a radioactive source or latent volcanic activity? Scientists construct geothermometers based on the elements found in samples taken from each of the springs. Elements range from flourine which tends to indicate deep circulation within the earth's crust to strontium, an element found in radioactive decay. These two elements would be present in water that is extremely hot, while an element such as silica would be present in an aquifer retaining a cooler temperature. The elements tell a story of rock layers and the geologic history under our feet.

While the chemical composition of atoms may give clues to the source of the water, scientists also point to dissolved solids as showing us the path that the water may have followed to the surface. Many of our thermal springs have high concentrations of calcium, carbonate and sodium. Calcium carbonate, as the glue in sedimentary rock, would indicate the water passed through sandstone or limestone. Sodium would speak of water that has circulated to a deep level in rock with a fine grain.

Many thermal springs have a high mineral content, sometimes beneficial, sometimes not. Most of the thermal springs in Arizona have favorable concentrations of sodium, lithium, potassium and chloride.

James Witcher writing for the Arizona Geology Society points out that the springs found on the Colorado Plateau tend to have a lower mean temperature

Thermal Springs
with degree of heat
1 - Warm Spring / 79
2 - Pakoon / 86
3 - Cluster, incl. Arizona / 145
4 - Lava / 90
5 - Colorado Pool / 86
6 - Oatman & Caliche / 90 + 79
7 - Frost Mine / 72
8 - Warm spring / 72
9 - Warm Spring / 81
10 - Tom Brown Spring / 82
11 - Cofer / 97
12 - Kaiser / 99
13 - Warm spring / 72
14 - Castle / 115
15 - Mitchel / 79
16 - Agua Caliente / 102
17 - Radium / 140
18 - Quitobaquito / 90
19 - Agua Caliente / 90
20 - Monkey / 82
21 - Antelope / 79
22 - Lewis / 68
23 - Astin / 75
24 - Hooker & N-O / 127 + 73
25 - Agua Cal. & Mercer / 86 + 77
26 - Soda / 75
27 - Warm spring 72
28 - Verde Hot spring / 104
29 - Tonto Natural Bridge / 72
30 - Hot Spring / 99
31 - Roosevelt Dam / 118
32 - Salt Bank / 78
33 - Warm Spring
34 - Warm Spring / 83
35 - Cassadore / 73
36 - Warm Springs / 86
37 - Coolidge Dam / 99
38 - Mescal / 84
39 - Pioneer / 91
40 - Warm / 79
41 - Warm / 90
42 - Indian Hot Spring / 118
43 - Grapevine / 90
44 - Eagle Creek / 97
45 - Clifton / 138
46 - Gilliard / 180
47 - New Mexico hot Springs
48 - Hannah Hot Spring / 132
49 - Frieborn Canyon / 92
50 - Salado / 72

Arizona's hot springs are popular with those who enjoy exploring the back country. With that comes one caution: Please respect the property rights of the landowners of the land on which the springs is located. If they do not wish to share the spring with the public, please do not attempt to enter their property without permission!

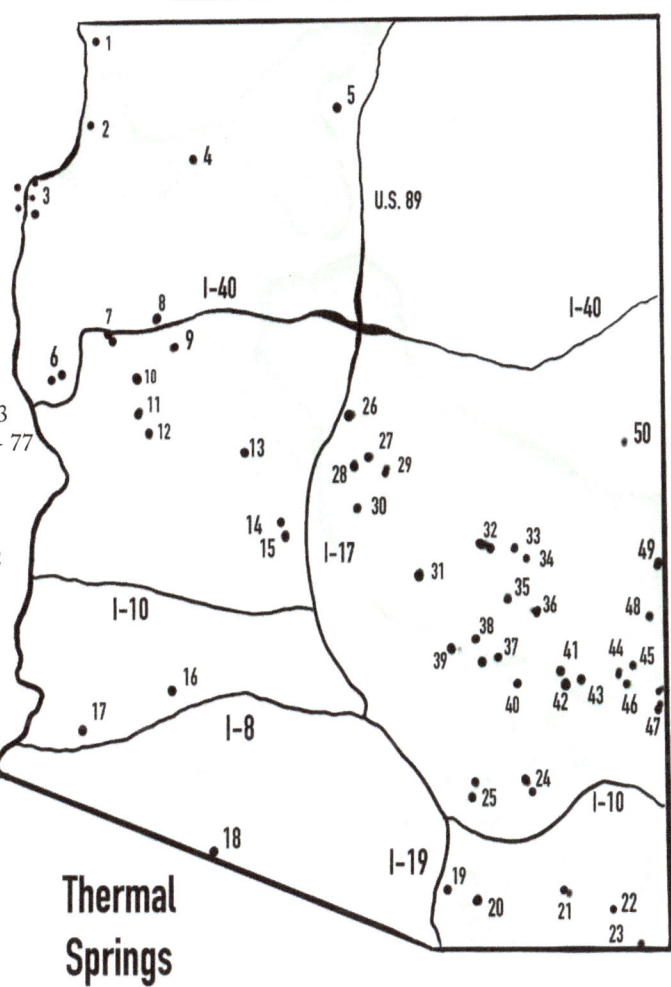

Thermal Springs

Source: American Geosciences Institute
https://www.americangeosciences.org/critical-issues/maps/thermal-springs-united-states

than those found in the Basin and Range region in southern Arizona, possibly indicating their proximity to bedrock. The area around Flagstaff and around Mount Baldy, both of volcanic origin, seem to have no hot springs. But when we look at the region around Yellowstone in Wyoming, we see numerous hot springs associated with a magma dome unlying the region. We can conclude that volcanic magma plays only a minor role in Arizona's hot springs. Witcher also notes that with some of our thermal springs' moderately warm temperatures may indicate that the hot water has mixed with cool water from a secondary aquifer.

The early Native Americans recognized that the warm waters were useful in treating injuries, whether muscular-skeletal or soft tissue wounds. Both Castle and Indian Hot Springs were used by the Apache and other tribes for medicinal purposes.

> **Thermal Spring-Loving Amoebas**
> Along with dissolved solids, scientists find amoebas, a single cell eukaryote, living in thermal springs. While some forms of amoeba are benign, the Naegleria Fowleri amoeba can cause cerebral meningitis. This little one-cell creature loves water heated between 77 to 104 degrees which is the same temperature range that most humans enjoy as well. One comforting thought is that this amoeba tends to live in water low in sodium levels.
>
> A second concern is the Legionella bacteria that is known to live in warm water. Both of these may give us pause as we hurry toward our favorite hot spring.

Castle Hot Springs

The discovery of Castle Hot Spring came as the US Cavalry was pursuing three native warriors in 1867. Colonel Charles Craig, the commander at Fort Whipple near Prescott, had received a report from a prospector of the tracks of a large band of native warriors moving along the southern flanks of the Bradshaw Mountains. Colonel Craig ordered two troops of US Cavalry to mount up and pursue the band of Apaches.*

When a scout found the trail, the Cavalry quickly set up an ambush. Fifty warriors appeared, moving single file. Colonel Craig ordered his 200 troops and scouts to 'shoot first, ask questions later!' Most of the warriors were killed in the melee but three escaped and disappeared over a ridge.**

The next morning, the Cavalry began searching for the three men. As they topped a small saddle, the sun rose, shedding light across the foothills of the

---

* At the the time, the Yavapai people were called Apache along with the Tonto Apache though the two tribes are of separate ethnic origin.
** Colonel Craig was severely reprimanded for the attack on the native warriors and transferred to Fort Churchill, an obsolete military garrison with only a guard station. Public sentiment had begun to change from the early days when the order of 'Shoot First' was deemed acceptable.

Bradshaw Mountains. In awe, the men reported that the hills looked like battlements and towers of an ancient castle. Lured on by smoke rising from a peak, they came to a stream and rode on to discover the source. The water tumbled down a rock face in a narrow canyon, flowing through a series of pools. Steam rose from the pools in the morning light. The stream was lined with cottonwoods and mesquite, the lower watercourse filled with reeds. The shade of the trees granted the trail-worn soldiers a respite in the shade. They named the stream Castle Creek for the morning light illuminating the foothills. I choose to believe that for a moment, the men forgot to look around for the natives they sought as they swung from their mounts. They must have knelt by the water, exclaiming as the warm current swept over their outstretched hands. The twitter of birds in the trees gave them a sense that this was a refuge.

When the Cavalry returned to Prescott, word quickly spread of the hot springs. Prospector Abraham Peeples and his wife Mollie would also claim to have discovered the spring but it was resident Tom Holland who first filed claim to the site. He built several crude cabins near the creek and charged admission to those seeking healing from the mineralized water. The property changed hands several times. Over the years, two large lodges were built for the guests.

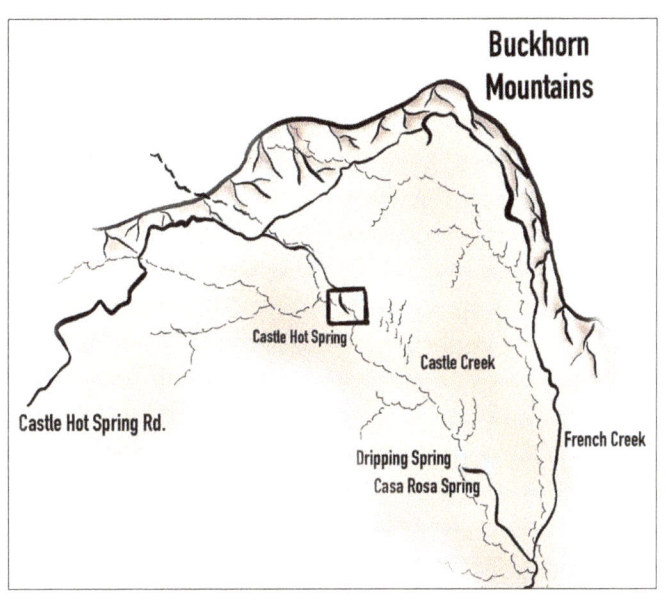

Once the guests were installed in the comfortable rooms of the lodge and soaking in the warm water, they must have congratulated themselves on their foresight to seek treatment at the springs in the Arizona desert.

Prescott was the official capitol for Arizona but for a few years, Castle Hot Springs became the defacto winter capitol. The first telephone line was installed from Prescott to the lodge at the spring. Washingtonia palms replaced the natural cottonwood and mesquite. The pools were lined with rock and advertizing was placed in the newspapers along the eastern seaboard, summoning patients for the cure. Despite the long trip, wealthy clients arrived and several wealthy families built their own homes on the property. In 1889, the Arizona Republic carried an advertizement for Castle Hot Springs, advertising lodging at $15. a week for guests. Miners were given lodging and meals for $10. a week.

During World War II, John F Kennedy recuperated at Castle Hot Springs from wounds received during his exploits in the Pacific as he led raids against the Japanese-held installations. An American flag is authorized to fly day and night from Salvation Peak over the resort due to his temporary residence.

By the late 1950s, the resort fell on hard times. In 1967, a fire broke out in the Palms Lodge, sparked by an unattended candle placed near the curtains of an open window. With the destruction of the lodge, the resort closed. A succession of caretakers tended the property and tried to keep four-wheeling trespassers from soaking in the pools.

The Yavapai and Tonto Apache were the first to recognize the medicinal qualities of Castle Hot Spring.

Then, in 2014, Mike Watts and his partners purchased the property with the intention of restoring the 'Grande Dame' of Arizona resorts. Today the property is a beautiful, exclusive resort concentrating on wellness, tucked away in a niche between rocky peaks with green lawns, verdant gardens and jade-tinted thermal pools. Guests drive out on a road along Castle Creek. The pavement turns to gravel soon enough and winds through a rocky desert canyon. Like earlier times, guests may question where they are headed as they cross a wash adrift in loose sand. The wash has been known to flood after a torrential monsoon.

The region around Castle Creek is ancient granitic and shist deposits overlain by basalt and rhyolite. Volcanic flows and rough breccia overlay the basalt. A graben fault on the northern margin with a second fault further south have broken and shifted the rock layers, providing a path for a deep aquifer to rise to the surface.

We can look to the Bradshaw Mountains rich in granite, gneiss and shist deposits when we consider the size of the aquifer. The forests at the summit speak of rain from moisture-laden clouds. The water from Castle Spring is clear and fresh tasting, filtered through thousands of feet of rock layers.

Over a 24-hour period, 200,000 gallons emerge at around 120 degrees fahrenheit. Analysis of the water shows a strong presence of sodium, chloride and sulfate. A small amount of lithium has also been found in tests run for the resort. The concentration of sodium and other elements, including chalcedony, would indicate that the water is released from an aquifer exposed to deep bedrock.

Volcanic activity in this region is considered to be fairly ancient and unlikely to be a source of heating for this aquifer. Rather than a radioactive or volcanic source of heat, scientists believe the water rises from a depth of over 10,000 feet. Based on a geothermometer, the temperature for this deep aquifer may be as high as 212 degrees fahrenheit with the heating from the earth's mantle. The testing indicates that the hot water may travel laterally for a distance or mix with water from a shallow, cooler aquifer before emerging onto the surface.

Verde Hot Springs is another popular site in central Arizona. Visitors to Fossil Creek frequently take the side trip to sit in a pool heated to just over 100 degrees, that was once part of the old resort.

Indian Hot Spring

In the early 1900s, a second spring favored by native tribes also became a haunt for those seeking the cure from mineralized waters. Indian Hot Springs is located about 20 miles north of Safford on the north bank of the Gila River flood plain and at one time produced 264 gallons rich in sodium-chloride ladened water per minute.

Ben Gardner was the first to channel the waters of Indian Hot Springs. The Apaches had been confined to Fort Thomas a few miles north and he thought he could safely develop the potential of the spring. Gardner was the first to channel the water through a pipe into a small pool. He sold the property to John Halladay and his son who in turn sold the spring to brothers John and Andrew Alexander.

The brothers took time off from running their store and stagecoach route in Globe to erect cottage tents and excavate a pool that measured 70 feet wide by 255 feet long. Their plans were the talk of the Gila Valley. The brothers did not disappoint local residents as they sponsored a valley-wide party before they officially opened the spa for business. Over 600 people came from as far away as the towns of Globe and Miami, each paying $1.75 to enjoy a day of games, music and dancing, food and swimming.

Once the property opened on April 21, 1903, the daily rate rose to $9.60. The springs quickly became popular, drawing patrons from across the country. The springs were located just off Highway 70 and the automobile allowed our populace to travel some distance from their homes.

The pool was expanded to 270 feet and lined with cement. The brothers built a three-story hotel for those who stayed more than a day. By 1916, the brothers' interest had moved on to new enterprises and they sold the property to Henry and Rose Hill. The Hills added private bath houses, a diving board and swing. The springs were very popular with the local population, as the Hills hosted school field trips and family outings.

Beginning in 1920, the property was sold once again but each owner seemed to quickly move on. The years were not kind to the old resort and in 1964, Jerry Hancock bought the property as a residence for his family. He was interested in raising cattle. His wife and sons continued to charge admission to the pool until 1966. The State of Arizona Health Department then determined that the family must begin adding chlorine to the pool and post lifeguards during open hours. The family closed the business and later sold the property to the Healing Waters Foundation. The resort faded into obscurity except for two small incidents that drew the attention of law enforcement.

> **Healing Waters?**
> With 220 parts per million of sodium and a trace of lithium, the native tribes may have found the spring comforting to sore muscles and joints as well as aiding in the healing of old wounds. In the 1950's, tuberculosis patients thought the dry air and warm water helped in their recovery.

In 1998, Royce and Regina Richardson along with Darrel Cope and his sons decided to take possession of the property and forced the caretaker to leave at gunpoint. The couple intended to use the springs as a private resort while commercially bottling the water for sale and raising medicinal herbs. The matter was settled in court when they were found guilty of forcible entry and the property was returned to the Indian Springs Corporation.

Again in 2002, law enforcement became involved with an Earth First Conference held at the springs. As the conference drew to a close, one attendee drew a gun and shot another man before committing suicide. Six years later, on the evening of February 24, 2008, the old hotel caught fire and burned. Local fire companies were unable to save the building. The caretaker was uncertain as to who had been on the property at the time of the fire though wet footsteps and clothing were found near the pool. The burned building was subsequently reduced to a pile of rubble and the property ruled off-limits.

In 2018, we inquired about visiting the springs - our inquiries went unanswered. We stopped by to see if we could find a way into the springs, preferably by legal means. We found a locked gate. A third party told me the family that owns the spring wishes to keep the property private. I was left with nothing more than the the wish that the spring could be restored and opened to the public again.

The Springs of the Gila

Indian Hot Springs is just one of the thermal springs found in the region around the Pinaleno Mountains. This range lies north of Interstate 10 and west of Safford, following the southeast to northwest regional alignment. The Pinolenos rise to 7,000 feet in elevation and receive around 30 inches of precipitation a year. The core of the range is primarily metamorphic rock consisting of fine-grain granite and basalt that formed deep under the earth's surface. On either side of the Pinolenos large basins have formed, filled with sediments that have washed down the slopes of this range. The Safford Basin is estimated to be up to 4,000 feet deep in sediment. While the Pinoleno range may be primarily metamorphic rock, surrounding areas show evidence of volcanic activity, primarily in the Peloncillo range on the eastern edge of the Safford basin. Two major faults run southeast to northwest along the Safford Basin. Smaller graben faults cross or branch off these two larger faults.

> From the
> **Bisbee Daily Review**
> August 31, 1910
>
> **Magnesium spring**
> *81 degrees,*
> **Iron and Mud Spring**
> *116 degrees,*
> **Rock Springs**
> *118 degrees and*
> **Beauty Spring**
> *119 degrees.*
>
> *All available to treat rheumatism, dropsey (edema), liver and kidney ailments, blood diseases and women's ailments. Fishing Pond, with lawns for tennis and croquet available.*

North of the Peloncillos, the Gila and San Franciso Rivers emerge from the Gila wilderness. The San Francisco is the largest tributary of the Gila which crosses Arizona to enter the Colorado River just north of Yuma. The San Carlos Reservoir now retains much of the water along the Gila for recreation and irrigation.

The region along the Gila and San Francisco rivers is rife with springs, including a number of thermal springs. The Safford basin is reported to have four geothermal reservoirs lying four thousand feet below the surface. Underlying these four are three more aquifers rated with moderate to high temperatures around 8,000 feet deep. The Peloncillos show a relatively recent history of volcanism. However, as the river enters Arizona, one stretch flows over bedrock. With the presence of sodium and chloride along with the depth of the aquifers, this could all indicate that heat radiating from the earth's mantle is heating the aquifer. One study by the Arizona Geology Survey suggests that the subsurface temperatures could be as high as 300 degrees fahrenheit.

Indian Hot Springs is one of the warmer thermal springs with temperatures between 113 to 118 degrees and a notable level of sodium and chloride. But this is not the warmest spring in the area. Gillard spring bears that honor, with a temperature of 176 to 183 degrees. The water has a high chloride content. Scientists believe that the Gila has cut through alluvial sediments down to bedrock where a fault brings the water to the surface. According to a report for the Arizona Geological Survey, a keystone graben fault near Gillard may control the geothermal activity throughout this region.

One scientist working with the Arizona Geological Society suggests that the thermal hot springs through this region may be the remnant of a much larger thermal system that no longer exists.

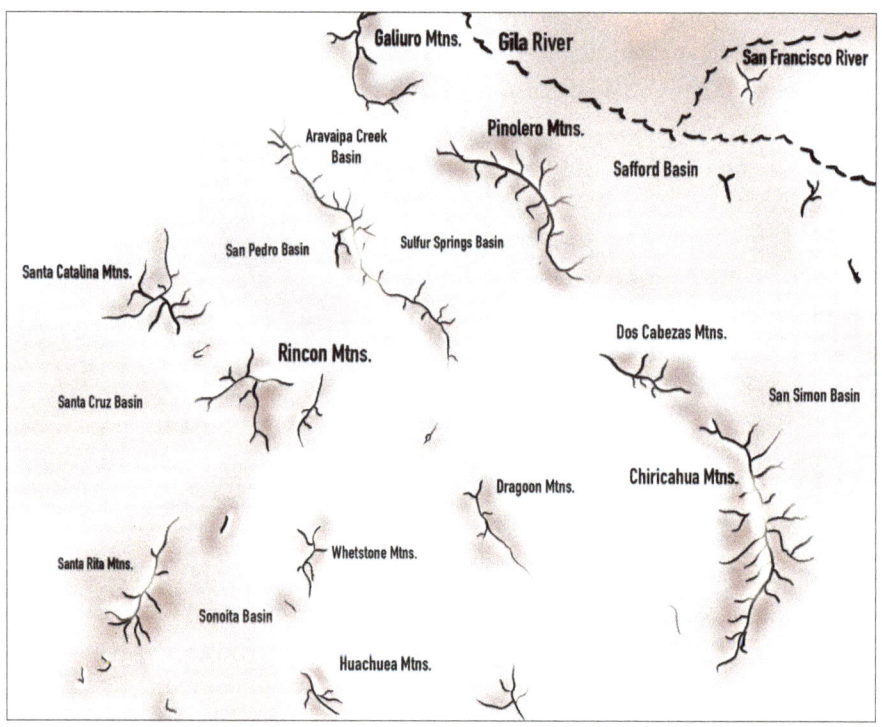

This map shows how large basins have formed between the mountain ranges of southern Arizona. Note how the range and basin geomorphology follows a southeast to northwest direction. The major faults align with this pattern as well.

Clifton Hot Spring

In examining the rock layers under Clifton, geologists find old rocks overlaying younger rocks with volcanic intrusions, all presenting a geologic puzzle. The San Francisco River flows out of the Gila Wilderness into the Gila River. The river

Thermal spring in 2015, prior to dewatering.

Roper State Park Thermal Spring

The region around Clifton and Safford has a number of hot springs. One of these was found in Roper State Park on the outskirts of Safford. The pool had been modified several times and most recently sat on a ledge next to a small restroom. Like many of the thermal springs, the water was laced with sodium and chloride, often useful in treating sore muscles and aching joints.

At one time, the water may have risen to the surface along a natural conduit, but in recent years, the water came from an artesian well located nearby. In 2019, the walls of the well collapsed and the water ceased to flow. Experts were called in, but the State Park concluded that the cost of a new well was beyond their resources. The pool was permanently closed and filled in to keep visitors from stumbling into the cavity. Whether the collapse was due to a receding aquifer, or the walls of the well were simply unstable, is unknown.

has worn its passage down to bedrock and intersects a fault that produces 102 degree water rich in sodium chloride. Drilling near the site, revealed both a warm and cool aquifer beneath the surface. The cooler aquifer lies at about 600 feet while the heated aquifer is over 1,000 feet below the surface. The waters travel 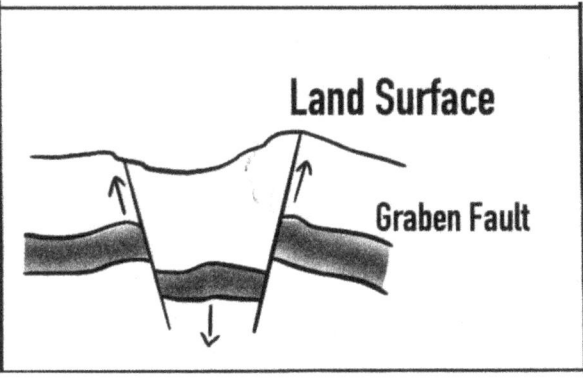 laterally, mixing, to emerge as if from one source. A keystone graben beneath the San Francisco River is believed to control the geothermal activity.

The spring was first described by a trapper, James Pattie, in 1825. Over the years investors thought the springs might be used for a health resort but success in their investments never materialized. Instead, the mines became the financial foundation for Clifton until the copper market dropped below a profitable level of return. In 2005, flooding covered the outlet of the springs under a thick layer of coarse gravel.

Hooker Hot Spring

When I first began researching the thermal springs, I was intrigued by the idea that thermal springs had emerged on the western, eastern and southern exposures of the Pinoleno Mountains. Could this mean that the Pinolenos still retained a source of magna near the surface? No, the range has a metamorphic core. However, Hooker Hot Springs on the western exposure may have a link to volcanic activity.

Hooker Hot Spring is located in Hot Springs canyon off of the southern tip of the Galiluro Range. The subsurface around the hot springs consists of thick layers of volcanic tuff interspersed with thin layers of conglomerate resembling cobble stones. The conglomerate swept down the Galiluros and Winchester ranges between volcanic eruptions. In Bass Canyon, just north of the hot spring, dark basalt boulders create a contrast with the lighter layers of rock formed from volcanic ash. Underlying these layers of volcanic deposits is an older layer of rhyolite around 2,700 feet below the surface.

Intersecting these layers is a fault that lies along the the west side of the basin at the foot of the Galiluro Mountains. The fault may be the conduit for the hot spring. Along with the hot spring, nearly 20 cool water springs emerge from a shallow aquifer caught in the alluvial deposits.

Hooker Hot Spring is not easy to access. We drove north from Interstate 10 along the base of the Pinolenos. The heights rise in stunning ramparts, outlined against a brilliant blue sky. I could only imagine a desert storm striking the rock

overhead with multi-million volt flashes of lightning. On this day, however, the harsh light left the land glaringly exposed without a sign of civilization other than the dirt track carved between stands of cactus. The miles passed, a trail of dust marking our passage.

As I questioned how a lush oasis could lay anywhere in this scarified landscape, a narrow strip of cottonwood appeared far from the track we followed. In time, the road began to dip between low hills. At last, a change comes to the terrain that could portend a watercourse ahead. The road dropped along a steep gradient into a canyon filled with brush and towering ash and cottonwood trees.

The small pond at Hooker Hot Springs is a refuge to Spotted Leopard frogs

This is the sanctuary of the Nature Conservancy and the home of Muleshoe Ranch.

In the late 1870s, Dr. Glendy King purchased the land around a cluster of springs at the foot of the Galiluro Mountains. He established a spa that would draw visitors from the east to enjoy the mineral-laced water as he treated their ailments. His plan came to naught when Dr. King was shot and killed by a neighbor in a land dispute.

After his death, the ranch was purchased by Henry C. Hooker, who steadily bought out other landowners until his ranch, the Sierra Blanca, spread over 800 acres. Dr. King's land would have been a valuable addition due to seven perennial streams and 20 springs on the property. The grasslands at the base of the Santa Teresa and Galiluro Mountains offered good grazing, and Hooker imported well-bred cattle to improve his stock.

A century later, when the Nature Conservancy purchased the property, the Directors renamed the property 'Muleshoe Ranch.'

As we drove toward the entrance to the ranch, I was astonished by the native vegetation that formed a thick barrier on either side of the

No Trespassing

At the insistance of the Nature Conservancy, let me make this very clear. If you are looking to casually slip into a pool of hot water to soak for an hour or two, Muleshoe Ranch is not open to the general public. The original buildings with four cottages are open to members of the Nature Conservancy by reservation only.

road to the point of feeling as if a green wall was pressing in upon us. We caught a glimpse of fully canopied cottonwoods towering over a low building, enclosed by desert hillsides. I began to exult in the presence of water, eagerly anticipating what we would find.

Leaving our car in a small parking area, we walked along a nature trail at the foot of a low ridge. Ahead the trail dipped into deep, loose sand, crossing a wide wash. Tall cottonwoods lined the banks with flood debris strung through the underbrush. I questioned whether the height of the trees was due to a shallow aquifer nurturing the growth or just a matter of surviving over a hundred years?

A mesquite bosque filled the understory. Vines lay thick, twisting over stumps and old tree skeletons. The whine of mosquitos and the gloom of a narrow canyon late in the day urged us onward.

The wash did not contain pools, not even a slow trickle of water but it was evident that a flash flood had swept the watercourse recently. Such a flood might strand a hiker on the opposing bank. The trail wound past a small pool, a habitat for endangered leopard frogs. At Muleshoe, the Conservancy is working to restore the landscape, with an emphasis on improving the seven streams that wind through the ranch.

Controlled burns are part of this process. When fire thins the under story, more water enters the aquifers below the surface and the springs above. The rivulets of water between the pools are growing, the current more evident. Within the streams, the number of pools are increasing and creating a better habitat for the Gila chub. Vegetation is allowed to overhang the streams giving the Gila chub dark pockets in which to hide from predators. Watercress is returning to the shallow backwaters. All of this speaks of restoration, of rebirth.

Once cattle crowded the banks of the streams, their hooves obliterating stream-side vegetation and churning the mud into the pools of water. The Nature Conservancy has reduced the number of cattle held on the land, giving it an opportunity to be restored to a healthy ecosystem.

While we did not find water in the wash, the abundant vegetation bore witness to the aquifers under the surface. The restoration of the property will benefit the springs in the long run as well as the species that live within this riparian zone.

Agua Caliente

Agua Caliente, translated as hot water, is a popular name for thermal springs across the southwest and one such spring is found in a Tucson city park. Driving across the desert plains toward the park in 2018, we caught a glimpse of Washingtonia palms sweeping the blue sky. Palms trees with their graceful fronds were once the iconic symbol of a spring and thrive in a desert region with subsurface water.

Agua Caliente Lagoon & Spring, Tucson

As we entered the park, we found a man-made lagoon, lined with shaggy palms and water reeds. Ducks, squabbling over territory, took flight skyward with
outstretched wings. Like any oasis, the abundance of water and green vegetation seemed unreal after crossing miles of dry desert.

Agua Caliente spring is located just a few steps from the parking lot. A small pool of brackish water marked the outlet, surrounded by sun-blasted bare dirt. A shallow ditch stretching from the spring to the lagoon was dry.

White settlers first came to Tucson following the war with Mexico. Homesteader Peter Bain first established a homestead at Agua Caliente. He found pottery chips and arrowheads indicating the spring had been used for thousands of years, most recently by the ancestors of the Tohono O'odham people. Bain soon sold his claim to James Fuller who planted an orchard and brought in a herd of cattle. He began advertizing the mineral-laced waters as a cure for rheumatism and kidney ailments. Twice a week he would drive clients from Tucson to his ranch in a horse-drawn wagon

Natural pool near Agua Caliente Spring

where they would spend two days soaking in the spring. After eight years, Fuller sold the homestead.

When first discovered, two springs emerged just a few yards apart, one with hot mineralized water, the other with cool water. In the 1930s, Gib Hazard, the current owner, decided to dynamite the entrance of the springs, hoping that the two would combine to increase the flow. The blast did not have the results he sought! Where once the springs had produced 500 gallons of water per minute, the flow was now reduced to between 150 to 300 gallons per minute of 72 degree water.

In the 1950s, the property was owned by Art Filiatrault, his wife and four children. The ranch had expanded through private aquisition to almost 1,200 acres. The original three pools had been expanded to seven pools and the family began to raise alfalfa for their cattle, increasing the demand on the aquifer. The family remodeled and expanded the ranch house into a gracious home that now serves as a Visitor's Center. Docents are present to answer questions and give a tour of the kitchens and living room.

In 1959, Art Filiatrault sold the property to a development company. A second attempt was made to increase the spring flow by blasting the outlet but once again the effort failed, decreasing the flow to between 100 to 125 gallons per minute. Fortunately, the plans to build a subdivision on the site did not proceed. In 1984, Pima County acquired the site and developed the Roy P. Drachman Park.

As Tucson continued to grow, more wells were drilled and in 2000 the spring stopped producing water. As the winter storms returned in 2001, the spring again produced a small flow. By 2002, the flow was measured at 47 gallons per minute, a mere trickle of what had once emerged. Of the original seven ponds, only three ponds remained and by 2018, the third pond was dry.

In 2016 Pima County used funds from a flood control grant to convert the second pond into three pools, removing palms trees and planting native vegetation. Lining the pools has helped to reduce the amount of water lost to seepage into the substrata. When Pond 1 is renovated, the cattails and non-native vegetation will be removed. The pond will be reduced in size with a a cienega creating a boggy area available to wildlife.

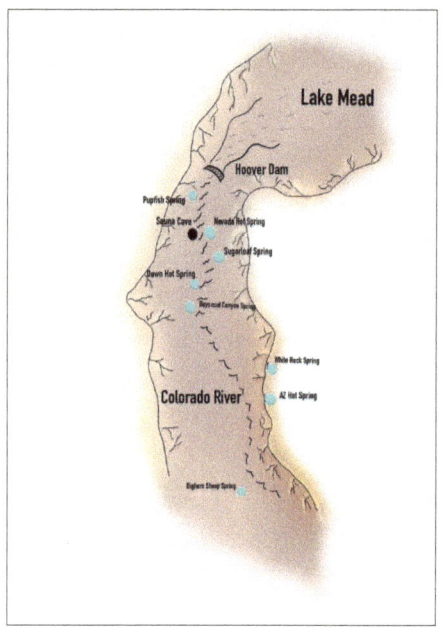

Ringbolt to Kaiser Hot Springs

The Black Canyon of the Colorado River, from the border with Nevada down to Willow Beach, has a number of hot springs. These springs draw hikers from inland trails and kayakers from off the Colorado River.

In the past, the region was volcanically active as part of the Kaiser Springs-Elephant Head Volcanic Zone. The canyon only receives about five inches of rain a year with a couple of inches more on the Eldorado Mountains, to the west. A study was done to determine the source of the aquifers feeding the springs due to the plan to build a housing development in the Eldorado Valley. There was some concern that wells for the development would negatively impact the springs and the riparian pockets so important to wildlife in this dry and rocky land.

The tests found the region on either side of the river was volcanic rock with pockets of alluvial sediment. The rock of the Eldorado Valley is mostly sedimentary. Scientists then asked if a series of faults and channels might bring water from the Eldorado Valley to the Colorado River. The consensus was no, as the alignment and angle of rock with volcanic dikes seemed to block any such channel. Nor did the chemistry align in samples between the two locations. Only Bighorn Sheep Spring seemed to channel water with the same atomic equation as the Eldorado Valley.

Of the springs further north, the cluster around the dam bore the atomic signiture of water in Lake Mead. Those springs futher south, beginning with

Palm Tree Spring, led geohydrologists to conclude that the water must filter through cracks in the volcanic rock into shallow aquifers.

What of the heating source? Shallow aquifers would usually not be effected by heating deep within the earth so geohydrologists speculated that the water might circulate through deep fractures and back to the surface. With the Nevada springs, a second theory involved the Boulder City pluton formation as a heat source. Chemical tests indicate that the temperature of the reservoir sending water to the surface at Ringbolt, near Nevada Spring may be as high as 160 degrees. The sodium-rich water has cooled to below 100 degrees when it reaches the surface.

Hot Spring along the Colorado River with sandbags forming a pool.

This is similar to Kaiser Hot springs off of US 93, south of Kingman. The water at Kaiser is rich in carbon dioxide, emerging out of a layer of course breccia. One study says it is common to find these elements along the borders of active volcanic geothermal activity.

These springs have been studied for geothermal power production, but no major investments have come forward to develop the potential. This may be due to the limited size of the geothermal systems as they currently exist.

The Desert Springs

The classic image with a desert spring is of a man crawling across heated sand. His hands and knees are blistered. He collapses at the edge of an palm-lined oasis, hand outstretched, begging for a cool sip of water.

Maybe this is a bit dramatic but then, have you visited the Mohave desert north of Lake Mead? As we crossed the Virgin River, I noted the dry hills beyond the wide line of brown water. The land is dotted with sagebrush and sparse blades of grass sought by both tortoise and cattle that live in this dry country. A few miles further, the grass has disappeared and trails of dust speak of all-terrain vehicles speeding along drought-stripped dirt tracks. These trails are the only sign of life other than a raptor riding the wind currents high overhead.

Whitney Pockets rises like a mirage on the horizon. Irregular sandstone formations dot the landscape, extending an invitation to explore the monument created by the desert. We turned onto one more unmarked road and left Nevada, crossing the state line into Arizona. On the hill above is a small fire cabin that was built with the sole purpose of keeping an eye on a rancher that would burn the plain's brush to encourage the grass to grow. The residents of this sparce and dry land are a tough breed, opposed to government regulation.

Up, up, we followed a dirt track over a mountain pass. I had begun to think we would not find Pakoon Spring after spending the morning misled in the network of dirt tracks on the plain below. As the road twisted down from the pass, another desert basin stretched to mountains on the horizon. I questioned why anyone would think they could carve out a living in this desert with only the breeze to stir the sagebrush. Nothing else moves across the landscape. We drove round a bend and there before us rose a wall of green unlike anything I had seen in a bone-dry desert. Pakoon!

Pakoon spring rises within a desert wash, bordered on one side by the Virgin Mountains. We parked near a fence intended to keep the wild burros out of the lush riparian zone. Ahead a lone cottonwood tree reached skyward, seemingly ambushed by brush with the limbs raised to the sky in petition for relief. Searching for evidence of standing water, I was startled to find beautiful white flowers floating across knee-high broad leaf plants, their presence silently proclaiming that water lays just below the surface. I studied this patch of meadow, wondering if I walked forward whether I would find mud oozing over my boots.

Pakoon spring

We worked our way around the edge of the vegetation, searching for some indication of open water. I could see a trace of water standing at the edge of a thick growth of eight-foot high reeds but hesitated to wade in. Small minnows flashed through the shallows. Then, I noted the rattlesnake posed on the edge of stream, patiently waiting for a meal. I pondered how the minnows could have appeared in this desert spring. For that matter, how could the reeds, the willows and the cottonwoods have found root here. Were the seeds blown in by the wind?

The thick swath of vegetation stretched down the slope for over a quarter mile as the wash narrowed between canyon walls. Washingtonia palms appeared further downhill. As we trudged along the edge it was evident that to support such a lengthy swath of vegetation, a large amount of water must flow from this spring. My partner and I were the only people present at that moment. No campers, no all-terrain vehicles. I was amazed as water is so rare in the desert. This spring continues to flow day after day, without human witness to an amazing creation.

We arrived at a small water weir a short distance down the slope. A researcher had torn great armfuls of water reeds from the watercourse to create a shallow pool for bats to scoop water mid-flight. Placed across the channel was a metal plate with a V-shape cut in the upper edge. As the water rose behind the plate, the current would begin to flow through the V-cut. The researcher could hold a one-liter container below the V-cut and time how many seconds, or minutes, it took to fill the container. Averaging the time from several attempts would indicate the volume of water flowing from the spring.

Pakoon had been the site of a ranch that raised both cattle and ostriches. Decades earlier, ranch hands had dug a channel from the spring to feed six ponds. The water from the ponds was used for irrigation and livestock. The rancher carved fields from the rocky soil north and west

Yerba Buena

of the spring to grow alfalfa.

The Bureau of Land Management acquired the ranch in 2004. Desert springs and the eco-system they form can be irreplaceable in such a dry landscape. The Bureau of Land Management formed a partnership with the Grand Canyon Wildlands Council, the Springs Stewardship Institute, and the National Park Service. The latter had an interest in the region due to their oversight at Lake Mead.

Jeri Ledbetter, Director of the Spring Stewardship Institute, explained one challenge in studying the spring: "In spite of the critical nature of water, particularly in arid climates, many springs remain unmapped. Land managers and conservation organizations cannot protect these ecosystems without the most basic information—their geographic location. What little information exists is fragmented and therefore largely unavailable to researchers, land managers, and conservation organizations."

Pakoon Springs is just one of 105 springs the group mapped in the Arizona Strip, one of the driest regions in the United States. With an agreement in place, the partners had an opportunity to learn whether this cluster of springs could be rehabilitated. Jeri thought that if the aquifer had not been depleted, there was a good chance that the springs would recover.

Water gauge

The site initally had around ten outlets, including several seeps. The most prolific outlets produced 130 gallons per minute, forming isolated pools below the spring

When researchers first arrived at Pakoon Spring, they found the land around the spring torn up by the tires of all-terrain vehicles. Old ranch buildings cluttered the site with decaying ostrich pens, scrap metal and tires, abandoned appliances and rusting vehicles. Much of the refuse was just junk, useless and discarded. Over the course of two years, with the help of volunteers, the partnership would haul over 100 tons, that's 200,000 pounds of refuse, off the site in large semi-trailers.

Once the refuse was hauled away, the invasive species and damaged terrain remained around the spring. One of the more vocal species that had multiplied at the spring were the bullfrogs. Their deep-throated croaks echoed off the hillsides in the evenings. Mosquitofish darted through the shallows. And there was one

Clem, the Alligator

For years, there had been rumors drifting through the Utah town of Saint George of an alligator at Pakoon Spring. The arid Mohave Desert is not the native habitat of an alligator. At times, speculation centered on the drinking preferences of those who claimed to have seen evidence of an alligator.

Pakoon Spring is an oasis in the far northwest corner of Arizona and was indeed the home of Clem, an American alligator. The reptile, less than 12 inches long, had first been given to Charles, the rancher, who owned the springs. As the reptile grew, Charles refused to believe that the alligator was dangerous. His dog thought otherwise. One evening, setting out to patrol the grounds before bedtime, the dog paused at the edge of the light shining from the door. Nose quivering, his ears raised to catch the slightest whisper. Then, tail between his legs, he bolted back into the trailer. The next morning, alligator tracks ringed the porch.

One afternoon, Clem sauntered up the driveway, passing a horrified ranchhand working beneath a pick-up truck. Clem paid no attention to the man. When fires rolled across the grasslands, friends joked about Clem being scooped up from the spring in a water basket beneath a helicoptor. All were relieved to learn the alligator had survived the close encounter.

When Charles sold the ranch to the Bureau of Land Management, he stipulated that the alligator was to be allowed to live out her life at Pakoon. Managers at the Bureau of Land Management knew the alligator could not remain in the desert spring.

Years later, Dr. Larry Stevens told me of the effort to capture Clem. Somehow the alligator managed to evade every trap set for her. Finally, the pools were drained and there was Clem, rumbling and hissing at the crew as they revealed her secret underwater cave. Larry Stevens dropped a snare over her head and pulled her ashore. She was loaded into a tank for a ride to her new home at the Phoenix Herpatology Society. When weighed, she was severely undernourished at 400 pounds.

Clem died several years ago, having reached a mature 800 pounds. A sign board at the spring honors her legacy at Pakoon.

more creature of whom rumors had spread throughout the years. For nearly 18 years an alligator prowled the spring, desperately searching for the next meal.

Over the next ten years volunteers chased and captured the bullfrogs, removing 1000 in 2001 and 725 in 2013. There was no way to completely eliminate the mosquitofish but managers hoped that with a return to a more natural setting, predators might be able to reduce the number of mosquitofish, and allow native species to multiply.

Volunteers pulled the thistles and tamarisks trees along with great swathes of cattails. When they finished, a barren, dry plain sat baking in the sun. The wind swirled the dirt in crazy patterns along what remained of the wash. In the next phase, a bulldozer contoured what had been alfalfa fields and large pens into a more natural water course that ran from a small rise on the north end of the wash toward the channel that disappeared on the south end between canyon walls. The partnership hoped the springs would emerge once again.

Cuttings from Gooddings willow, seep willow and Fremont cottonwood were shoved into damp soil as the spring began to recover. Bullrushes, salt grass

and Yerba mansa were introduced around the cuttings. The Yerba produces the white flowers.

In 2013, the flow of water was measured at 90 gallons per minute, an abundance of water in such a dry location. Then the winter of 2014 rolled in and high water swept through the wash, re-arranging all the earth-work that had been done. Many of the plantings were swept away. In their place the willows and the cattails multiplied. Managers decided that no further effort would be made to introduce the species wiped out by flooding.

After the reeds were established, spring snails, speckled dace and relict leopard frogs were introduced into the ecosystem. In the months that followed, observers found evidence that mammals were returning: rodents, including the kangaroo rat, coyotes, bobcats and big horn sheep all dropped in to quench their thirst. Four species of bats swept across an open stretch with low-flying passes. Quail and hawks, ravens, wrens and warblers, sparrows and gnat catchers all returned to the tall cottonwood and willows along the water's edge.

Like southern Arizona, the aquifers of this region are part of the basin and range terrain: steep rugged mountains divided by deep basins filled with alluvial deposits. We had crossed Lime Kiln Pass to drop into the small valley that contains Pakoon Springs. Could there be a deeper aquifer created by the tremendous faults found through this region?

Scientists do not have enough data yet to determine how the geology of this region retains the aquifers under the surface. There seems to be some indication that the water from the Grand Wash Cliffs moves south toward Lake Mead.

Campers may settle no closer that a quarter mile from the spring. The fence around the spring and upper riparian channel is intended to keep wild burros from moving in and tearing up the vegetation. As we drove back up the pass, I thought about the thousands of hours, the number of trips made over that dirt track in the previous 14 years to return an obscure spring back into a healthy ecosystem. What a treasure in such a harsh environment!

Sowats Point and the Esplanade

There is a second cluster of desert springs on the Arizona Strip that I first encountered around the time the partnership was starting the rehabilitation of Pakoon Spring. I had eagerly read of Kanab Canyon, a impressive side canyon of the Grand. I studied photos of pools at the base of steep canyon walls and rock pour-overs.

In the spring of 2005, my son and I pulled on our backpacks and began hiking down the Jumpup Trail onto the Esplanade. After three quarters of a mile through a shallow drainage, the trail emerges onto a ledge at the top of sheer 300 foot-high cliffs. The wind tore at the edges of our backpacks. Below us dust swept across an expanse of rock ledges and canyons, twisted and torn by upheaval and the forces of wind and water. It was spectacular and fearsome.

We crouched momentarily, waiting for the wind gusts to drop. I hate standing on the edge of a cliff and the gusts did not reassure me. In a quiet moment, I stepped out onto the ledge. The trail is about ten feet wide with a narrow verge at the edge of the cliff. I tried to keep from looking over the edge as I braced against the gusts. Far below I could see a lone cottonwood tree and the glint of water: a desert spring. I suddenly wanted to visit that spring and sit along the edge. The pool reflected the brilliant light as a mirror to the sky. I studied the pool at each bend in the trail, noting that little grew along the edges and the soil itself looked blighted. Only one sad tree bent over the water's surface.

The trail along the cliffs reached a point where it turned to descend along a steep, narrow path cluttered with rock ledges and loose stone. We crept down the talus pile. As we drew near the spring, the hint of sulfur reached us. No! A bitter spring. What a disappointment! I had no desire to sit in the sulfur-tinted fumes as I moistened my dry lips.

We returned to the trail, moving toward Jumpup Canyon. Our feet scuffed through dry sand as we raced the lengthening shadows of the late afternoon. Within a few short weeks my son would depart for his military service. We had only 24 hours to explore the canyon before we climbed the talus pile and cliffs to return home. I never forgot the promise and the disappointment of that spring.

In 2018, I returned with my husband. As we stood at hilltop, the temperature was starting to climb. I could not have known how difficult would be our return. Two hours later, having hiked just under three miles, we approached a cluster of cottonwood in a narrow wash at the base of the ridges that underpinned the talus pile. The descent had been difficult as we dropped over protruding ledges and skittered against loose rock. Ken kept protesting that we should not be in this canyon as temperatures climbed toward 100 degrees.

Unlike the previous venture, we did not find water in the spring. Ken questioned whether this was a spring but I was certain I had found a pool of water in that location 14 years earlier. I still had the photographs!

Overlooking the Esplanade, the small cluster of cottonnwood below is the sign of a spring.

As we approached the cottonwoods, not one whiff of sulfur reached us. We rested in the shadow of the trees as we ate our lunch. We had no time to waste as we began climbing back up the rim. The light was intense, the heat pressed down on us and rose from the rocks beneath our feet as if we were in an oven. We should have remained under the cottonwoods until evening but it was just under three miles back to the trail head. I would emerge ten hours later, alone without a

---

*Ten hours to walk six miles? The story of an hours-long struggle to survive is told in the book, *To Breathe Another Day*.

Large, mature cottonwood mark the presence of a spring, even when water is not present above ground.

light or water, one step at a time along Sowats Point.*

The spring we hiked to was one of a series of springs at the base of the Point. The canyon wall above the Esplanade is formed by sedimentary layers of sandstone over a layer of Hermit shale which in turn overlies the Esplanade sandstone. The Esplanade appears to be a massive stage above the inner gorge. Isolated juniper with clumps of desert grass rise from the sandy waste and rocky flats.

Returning after 13 years, the drainage below Sowats Point had changed. Several healthy clumps of cottonwood rose from a low ridge in Kwagunt Hollow. Each tree, at least 20 feet high with a healthy canopy of green leaves, seemed to celebrate the presence of subsurface water. The southwest has been caught in a drought for over 20 years, accounting for the absence of the pool. Overhead, a pocket beneath a pourover held dark green moss clinging to the pale sandstone wall as evidence of a seep. Could the pool I witnessed years earlier have simply been runoff that nurtured the trees? Or was there an actually up-welling of spring water along the fault lines that lay beneath Sowats Points?

There is a more philosophical question that lies in the desert sand at the base of the point. Often we have expectations of what we will find in exploring the outdoors. Seeing the designation of a spring on a back country map evokes images of a pool of cool water, and we begin to imagine the relief of dipping a handkerchief into the water. We anticipate running the damp cloth over a sweaty face and neck. We might even dip our head in the pool and peel off our dusty boots to soak our feet. We reflect on this image as we hike for miles with more miles yet to come.

And then, in 2003, there was that wisp of sulfur. Disappointment roared to life as the image of cool refreshment vanished into the thin air. How often in life do we encounter disappointment after hours of pleasant contemplation over what will come our way? That is the cruelty of a mineralized spring in a desert region. The promise dashed, our expectations unfulfilled. If we should be dangerously dehydrated, the disappointment comes with a blast of fury as we contemplate our possible demise.

The water of a mineralized spring is often from a distant past. Scientists talk of ancient water based on carbon-dating that may age the aquifer back thousands of years. Most highly mineralized water has emerged from deep underground. Through its passage, the water dissolves the minerals in the rock, taking on a

Looking back at the cliffs of Sowats Point.

mineralized taste, whether it be sulfur, sodium or some other element.

Looking at a map from the United State Geological Survey, we find Sowats Point is surrounded on either side by springs: Cottonwood, Upper and Lower Sowats and my favorite, Mountain Sheep Spring, lie on the northern exposure. I can imagine a hiker stumbling around a rock hoodoo and encountering a band of mountain sheep as they spring away from the pool of water at the unanticipated intrusion. I wonder about Cottonwood Spring, a pool seemingly large enough for the image to be captured by a low-level satellite. Did the cluster of cottonwoods indicate the water table emerging at the base of the cliff? Possibly this is a rheocrene spring with the water emerging in the channel.

Dr. Donald Bills has studied the geology of the Arizona Strip, spending long hours on the desert plateau. I asked him whether this was a spring or nothing more than runoff? He confirmed that intermittent springs appear at the base of the point and the beautiful green canopy of the cottonwood can be a marker of a spring.

Remarkably, both palatable and mineralized water seems to seep from the earth, indicating that there is more than one aquifer contributing to the pools when they are present. The pools, either fresh or mineralized, are in close proximity to each other.

The book of James in the Bible asks, "Can both fresh water and salt water flow from the same spring? Can a fig tree bear olives, or a grapevine bear figs? Neither can a salt spring produce fresh water."

Just as our words reveal the condition of our soul, so a bitter spring speaks of what lies beneath the surface of the earth, hidden in the rocks below our feet. As I considered the cottonwoods, the dry desert landscape and a pool of high mineralized water, I understand that water sustains life. When a spring is highly mineralized it may be unpalatable for humans to drink. A bitter spring in a desert is one of dashed hope, reminding us to consider what we should hold as most valuable in life.

What would we pay to preserve our lives? The next chapter tells the story of two men who asked that question. Both were hermits who relied on a spring; one found peace, the other revealed how twisted a man's mind can become.

The Hermitage

As our culture has advanced, we as a people find the land in which we live to be a water-desert. By this I mean that if we were deprived of our modern water works, we would be hard pressed to find a source of water beyond our urban setting. Imagine making the choice to turn your back on the comfort offered by civilization to live in the back country without modern utilities. Such a life would include an absence of water faucets!

The dictionary describes a hermit as a reclusive or solitary individual. Popular myth cloaks the hermit with a reputation for being at odds with society, preferring his own company to that of other people. In my research I learned of two such men who chose to live as hermits rather than remain in a comfortable home in a civilized setting. Each relied on a spring in the back country to provide the water for daily survival. Their stories are intriguing as we consider the narratives attached to the springs of Arizona.

In 1880, the description of a hermit was applied to Dr. Robert Neville. As settlers moved into Arizona, Dr. Neville seemed to prefer his own company, settling into a shallow canyon near, but not too near, Fort Rucker in the foothills of the southern Chiricahuas. He lived alone, emerging only to purchase needed supplies. Dr. Neville told the officers at Fort Rucker that he had built a small cabin. He listened carefully to their concerns about Apache raiding parties who periodically left the rocky folds of the Chiricahua Mountains. His choice to live alone earned him a reputation as the hermit of the Chiricahuas but few had ever visited his small camp.

In 1881, he met Sarah and John Lemmon as they lingered in southern Arizona during their honeymoon.* The couple were gathering botanical specimens which Sara carefully illustrated in her journal. Dr. Neville invited the couple to live in his cabin as they explored and collected specimens in the southern Chiricahuas. They were happy to be settled in a cabin with a roof over their heads.

As time passed, however, they began to suspect that Dr. Neville was not as mentally sound as they first thought. Sarah was concerned about reports that the Apaches were once again raiding camps along the border and she feared for their

---

* While in Tucson, Sara would become the first white woman to climb to the summit of the Chiricahuas. The peak we know as Mount Lemmon is named after her.

lives. When they mentioned their concern, Dr. Neville revealed a plan to blow the raiders to shreds with a lit match, a long cord and a keg of gun powder. He showed them a 125 foot-long tunnel he had dug into a ridge near his cabin. He planned to take refuge in the underground chamber during expected hostilities.

When a report of eminent activity came from nearby Fort Rucker, the Lemmons and Dr. Neville quickly moved to the underground chamber. The couple certainly did not expect to remain hidden in the 8 by 6 by 4 foot room for 11 days. By the time the Cavalry arrived to rescue them, the couple was more than relieved to escape the company of Dr. Robert Neville.*

A small rheocrene spring near the site of Neville's cabin

The road accessing Rucker Canyon and Neville's home crosses the southern Chiricahuas between the San Bernardino and the Sulfur Springs Valleys. A few old buildings still stand at the site of Camp Rucker and visitors can wander through the historic site.

The site of Dr. Neville's cabin and tunnel lies just off Rucker Canyon Road at the end of a dirt track so narrow, tree branches on either side pinstripe intruding vehicles. The track follows the base of a high ridge to a parking area near a lush meadow. At one time this may have been a hillside spring that fed a small pond. With the aquifer dropping, today the spring is more of a seep or possibly a hypocrene spring. The lush grass is knee high in a small depression. Nothing remains of the cabin that sheltered John and Sara Lemmon. The tunnel Dr. Neville dug into the ridge is hidden by brush. Only a few feet of it remain as much of the tunnel collapsed after Dr. Neville left the site.

* The Southwestern Legacy of Sara Lemmon, Wynne Brown, Arizona Highways Magazine.

The Chiricahuas are the result of successive periods of volcanic activity with the Turkey Creek Caldera being the largest contributor to the development of the range. When Turkey Creek erupted the explosion expelled so much rock and ash that the surface collapsed, creating a caldera 12 miles across. Beneath the volcanic rock lie older layers of sedimentary rock.

Camp Rucker is located south of the Turkey Creek Caldera. Around Rucker Canyon the hills are gentler than the steep slopes further north but still capable of producing flash floods along the canyons that wind between the hills.

Rucker Canyon dam and the the streem that flows through the infill.

A perennial stream once flowed down Rucker Canyon to the community of Whitewater. Today visitors driving through Elfrida would fail to guess the potential strength of the runoff in this little gulch. Camp Rucker was named for US Cavalry Lieutenant John Rucker who lost his life in a flash flood in the narrow canyon trying to save another soldier.

In the 1930s, the Civilian Conservation Corps built a dam across the upper canyon, creating Rucker Lake. Fishermen enjoyed some of the finest trout fishing in Arizona in the waters of this little lake.

My husband remembers fishing at Rucker Lake in the 1950s. As raindrops began to fall, his father would rush to the car, urging family members to hurry. He would race down the canyon, trying to outrun a potential flash flood that would have cut off their exit.

Today Rucker Lake no longer hosts fishing tournaments. After a huge wildfire swept over the southern Chiricahuas, monsoonal rains swept debris into the lake, filling the basin. The lake was restored only to have the same pattern happen a second time.

Today, visitors stroll across a sandy plain where clear mountain waters once provided a refuge to man and wildlife. A clear stream cuts across the plain to splash over the dam into the canyon below. The water caught in the grit and sand filling the basin provides a model for understanding the formation of an aquifer. A closer look at the dam shows a pipe installed at the base of the dam with a stream of water pouring into the rocky streambed. The basin has been transformed into an alluvial plain that will store a great deal of water within the sedimentary layers trapped behind the dam.

Before the fires there were springs high in the hills above Rucker Lake. I asked whether the debris from the fires would have disrupted the springs as they did the lake below? Would the sediment have buried the outlets so deep the water was unable to emerge? The general consensus by Forest Service personnel is that the springs will emerge. In Part III, we will look at what happened to the springs in Miller Canyon after another devatating fire.

The Hermit of Sycamore Canyon

In researching the springs of the northland, I met Jaybyrd, a man who had lived as a hermit in the northland's Sycamore Canyon just a few years ago. I once asked why he would choose to live separately from society in a daily struggle for survival without the comfort of a modern home. I came to learn that the springs of Sycamore Canyon meant far more to him than the water I so casually released into my kitchen sink at home.

Jaybyrd grew up in the neighborhoods of North Hollywood. He describes his dad as a man with outdoor skills who enjoyed backpacking and camping. At an early age, Jaybyrd came to respect his father's outdoor ethics, born out of his experience in the forest and desert.

By the time he entered his teens, his parents had divorced and Jaybyrd was spending a lot of empty time on the streets. At age 13, he was arrested for burglary. His mother took him to a counselor in an effort to turn her son from the path he seemed to favor. As he grew older, she sent Jaybyrd to live with his dad.

For a while, he seemed to make better choices, even attending a Christian college. After three years, he transferred to a community college seeking an education that would prepare him for some sort of lucrative career. Working in construction, he began to drift back to the streets and the drug scene that had drawn him in years earlier.

He told God, "I can't seem to get it together and I'm tired of being miserable. Until you show me who you are, I'm not going to pretend."

Jaybyrd bought a Harley. When he met a man cooking metamphetamines, he took up a route, distributing drugs through southern California. By age 22 he was once again in prison. With a wry smile, he says, "Better criminals don't get caught."

After getting out of prison, he went straight until his construction job vanished with an economic recession. Once again, he turned to dealing drugs. When he was arrested again, he was sentenced to a three-year stint in Chino Federal Prison. California had passed a law requiring any person convicted of three felonies to serve a 25-year sentence when convicted of a third offense. Jaybyrd had now racked up two felony convictions.

He decided it would be best if he left California and found a job flipping burgers just over the state line in Arizona. Jaybyrd was still using drugs and "playing the system." Despite considerable artistic talent, he thought he could not make a living as an artist. With a wry smile, as he says of his talent, "You have to be dead for a couple hundred years to make any money."

Instead, he turned his artistic talent to the tattoo industry. When I questioned how he learned to apply ink under the skin, he says, "The people I hung out with, we all liked tattoos. We just figured out how to do it." His arms were covered with dark ink, the hallmark of a tat man. Along with his new career, he was using heroin and speed.

After ten years, Jaybyrd knew that this was a lifestyle that would end poorly and he began looking for a way out. The police were pressuring him to become an informant. He refused and decided to move to the small town of Showlow where he set up a small tat shop. When the Chediski fire swept through the White Mountains four years later, his business disappeared with the flames. Jaybyrd returned to Flagstaff. He was becoming ever more desperate to give up the contraband drugs and poor choices. He began telling God that he wanted out but that he could not escape on his own.

God spoke, asking, "Do you really want out?"

Jaybyrd came to believe that he had two choices: remain in the lifestyle and society he had lived in for decades ... or he could move out into the wilderness.

In 2003, he heard God speak again, "Time to begin."

Jaybyrd shaved his beard and head. He gave away his remaining possessions. He was 50 years old and asking, "What is real? How am I to live?"

From his early years, he remembered the examples of other men who followed God into the wilderness. In February 2004, he loaded up a duffle bag with a large sleeping bag, a "crappy" tent, food, a Bible, and a pair of snowshoes. He had a map, a compass and cans of food. He admitted he knew nothing about Sycamore Canyon. A friend with a four-wheel drive jeep gave him a ride. They got within five miles of the rim before the snow became too deep to drive further. Before leaving him, his friend shook his head, saying, "Byrd, I really don't feel good about leaving you out here like this."

Stumbling a couple of miles through the open space between trees, Jaybyrd made camp for the night. As he lay there looking up at the stars, reality settled in. He had come front and center with himself.

The next morning he awoke, disoriented from the extreme change. No drugs, no traffic, no radio, no noise, no distractions, no job. He didn't need to protect his stuff, except from the marauding crows. Even as he struggled to accept the change, he felt as if he had stepped over a threshold and out of prison. He lay in the open, in the silence, relieved to have the weight off his shoulders.

Kelsey Spring

Later that day, Jaybyrd found another man who had taken up the life of a hermit. This man had built a camp well below the rim of Sycamore Canyon. He showed Jaybyrd the skills he needed to survive in a wilderness setting. Jaybyrd would spend the next five years in a hovel created from tarps and a tent spread over wood poles. Every few weeks he would make his way back to Flagstaff, either walking, or when available, catching a ride to buy groceries. A friend would give him a ride back to the rim. From there Jaybyrd would relay his supplies down to the camp.

Jaybyrd read book after book, seeking to understand his existence and to grasp the underpinnings of faith. Jaybyrd is a socially adept person. He chose to become a hermit to move beyond the distractions of our society, to concentrate on the One he believed had created all that Jaybyrd counted as life-giving and important.

The lifestyle of a hermit is alien to most people rushing though the hours of

Babe's Hole

work in a culture that encumbers us with expectations and material possessions. The life of a hermit reduces existence to the most important elements of staying alive. Desperation brought Jaybyrd into the wilderness where he would depend on a thin trickle of water for life.

There are no water lines in the wilderness. No water faucets. Without water, the human body cannot live much longer than three days. It would have been impractical for Jaybyrd to have hauled huge kegs of water out to his camp. As we consider how he would live under such primitive conditions, we understand that he would have returned in part to the days of the primitive tribes that once populated the valleys of central Arizona. Yes, he depended on modern society for food, clothing and a form of shelter but when it came to the water, life-sustaining water, he had to look to the source.

Sycamore Canyon was born out of a major cataclysmic event as faults separated, grinding rock against rock. Add the erosion caused by wind and water, the slide of rock pulled downward by gravity and the chasm widened. Meltwater and summer monsoons carried the soil and rock down the growing channels toward the Verde River. Along the canyon's rock walls, springs emerged out of the age-old stone.

Jaybyrd settled in a section of the canyon that lies south of the community of Parks, between Flagstaff and Williams. Several trails drop off the rim, following the terrain to the depths of the canyon and on downstream to the Verde.

Babes Hole, located in a grove of black walnut trees, became his most reliable spring. The spring is in a circular depression with the surface of the water well below the rim. Due to the depth of the water below the rim, the riparian zone is somewhat limited. Jaybyrd filled his collapsible plastic container below the water's surface till they were full. He found that he could carry one container in his backpack, the second in his arms the half mile back to his camp. He was stingy with each drop as he knew the labor required to obtain the water.

Compare Jaybyrd's meager supply of water, those few gallons hauled to a camp half a mile distant to what we squander in our modern homes. The average length of a shower runs 8.2 minutes and used 17.2 gallons at a rate of 2.1 gallons a minute. That accounts for 120 gallons a week of water usage compared to Jaybyrd's four to six gallons.*

He infrequently used two other springs. Kelsey Spring, a steep climb above Babe's Hole, could produce a small flow following a wet winter. Dorsey spring, much further away from the camp was almost not worth the effort as it dripped from a rock face. Filling any size container required patience during a long wait over a trickle of water.

The riparian zone extending below Dorsey follows a channel downhill. The soft earth displays the prints of deer and elk that come to the pockets of water caught in the channel. Damselflies dart across the muddy banks, chasing other small insects and the gnats swarm across a sweaty face. The spring is located in a small park with primitive campsites for hikers who explore the depths of Sycamore Canyon.

Kelsey Spring, being more productive, leaves deep mud along its channel, hidden by a layer of vegetation.

Dorsey Spring

My dogs were startled as their forelegs sank into the muck while their hind legs pushed from behind. Some years, the mud is deeper than others. An old pipe and tank bear witness to the spring being used to water sheep in years past.

We think of water as flowing so easily from the tap but Jay came to understand the close relationship between the water that filtered into the ground and the water than seeped from the spring. This was living in a harmony that our

* Home_water_works.org

modern society fails to recognize. We accept the gifts we are given so casually, assuming more will come our way when we need them. While Jaybyrd depended on the spring, he also understood that in a drought the spring might fail to produce enough water to supply what he needed to survive.

I don't know if he would still be living this hand-to-mouth existence. The morning came when he woke to a loud voice demanding his attention and the bore hole of a rifle ending in front of his face. Months before a hiker had felt threatened by a man who discovered her sitting at Dorsey Spring while she waited for her companion to return from the canyon depths. Frightened, she later reported the incident and the Forest Service with federal drug enforcement agents began looking for the man she encountered. They suspected he might be tending an illegal crop far from the eyes of law enforcement. Although Jaybyrd was not tending an illegal crop or paying unwanted attention to women hikers, he was still guilty of living in a permanent camp on the land under Forest Service jurisdiction which is illegal under federal regulations.

While the public may not pay much attention to the springs or a hermit taking up residence in the forest, disputes over the rights to the use of a spring have made the headlines in both electronic and print media. In the next chapter we'll look at several conflicts over the springs and begin to consider the legal code governing the use of our aquifers.

Bog Spring

Tucked in a fold on the western slope of the Santa Rita Mountains, Bog Spring is popular with both wild life and outdoor enthusiasts. It is found along one of the premier trails within Madera Canyon.

The water most likely rises from a perched aquifer. Giant sycamores tower over the spring box creating a quiet pocket overlooking the slope below. In the past, a bear sow and her cubs have roamed the slopes near the spring. Madera Canyon is a summer retreat for many species of birds migrating north during the warmer months of the year.

Dipping Vat Spring, Big Lake

Part III

Seeking the Commonweal

Hospital Flat Spring : A Refuge from Fort Grant

Wool uniforms in the desert's heat?

In the years before wicking fabrics and air conditioning, the heat could be brutal for the men in the US Cavalry. One of the earliest Cavalry camps, Fort Grant, was built in the lowlands west of the Pinoleno Mountains. The location offered no trees or desert stream to cool overheated men. When the heat and the stress of pursuing the Apaches became too much for a man to bear, the soldier was sent to Hospital Flat near a reliable spring in the Pinoleno Mountains. The cool air stirring the groves of pine, fir and aspen around the spring with a meadow of fresh, green grass made this an idea location to recover from deadly heat in the desert below.

Water Wars

The silence that settled over Apache Pass on the afternoon of July 15, 1862 should have caught the attention of the soldiers as they climbed toward a saddle. One moment a lone cicada buzzed, in the next a bullet sped past the ear of Private Johnson. He stumbled, uncertain of what had just happened. In that moment, all hell broke loose as hundreds of bullets poured from the hillside toward the thin line of 30 soldiers winding along the rocky wash. The soldiers quickly dropped to their knees, hugging any shelter close at hand, whether a large rock or cut creek bank.

"How many are there?" muttered Private Johnson. A groan seemed to be his answer from a pair of legs draped across a chunk of basalt.

"You okay, Murphy?" Johnson asked. Only silence responded.

In the weeks before the battle of Apache Pass, a Cavalry unit from the California Volunteers approached Tucson. The Cavalry, a forerunner of Union Forces, were assigned to challenge Company A of the Arizona Rangers, a Confederate force for possession of this crossroads town. Recognizing that they were significantly outnumbered, the Confederate Force chose to withdraw, without a fight from the town along the Butterfield Stagecoach route.

After arriving in Tucson, Col. James H. Carlton, the Commander of the Union forces pursued the Confederate Forces. He sent out 30 infantrymen and a 22-man Cavalry unit under the command of Captain John Cremony and Captain Thomas Roberts. The column included 21 wagons, 242 horses and mules along with 2 mountain howitzers. The howitzer is a cannon with a short barrel mounted on a two-wheeled axle that fires a projectile at a steep ascent to rain down a limited load of propellent onto the enemy. The howitzers would prove to be the critical element in the battle for Apache Spring.

The column left Tucson and crossed the San Pedro River, a perennial source of water. Captains Roberts and Cremony were reluctant to commit their entire column until they had determined whether there was sufficient water at Dragoon Spring to satisfy the men and livestock. An advance unit, including three wagons and seven cavalry officers, arrived at the spring to find a good flow of water and signaled the remaining men forward.

Apache Pass, located between the Dos Cabezas and Chiricahua Mountains, just south of the town of Wilcox.

The next morning, the regiment arose before dawn to cross the Wilcox Playa to the foot of the Dos Cabezas Range. Historically, the Playa collected runoff, creating a shallow body of water due to a layer of clay. Today, it remains dry most of the year.

Temperatures in July would have easily topped 100 degrees. The soldiers were outfitted with wool uniforms. Under the blazing summer sun, the men would have become overheated. The troops rolled across the Playa and into the foothills of Dos Cabezas, a distance of about 25 miles. Around noon, the column marched up the wash toward Apache Spring, anticipating the cool water that would quench their thirst and cool their heated bodies.

The Apaches under the leadership of Cochise and Mangus Colorado patiently allowed the soldiers to advance. Siphon Pass is the result of geologic upheaval with older limestone layers being thrust upward to overlay younger volcanic rock. Cross faults intersect a thrust fault running along a northwest to southeast course. Apache Spring rises along the Apache fault in a fold between two hills along Siphon Wash - a course the soldiers followed. The pass had long been a trade route between the Sulfur Springs and San Simon basins.

The Apaches had long recognized the value of the spring, and frequently camped near it. At first they shared the water with the white settlers. Then, in a misunderstanding, Army Major Bascom arrested the wrong Apache warriors for the kidnapping and death of a white child. In exchange for one life, the lives of three Apaches were taken. Cochise, one of the leaders of the Chiricahua Apaches,

From a memorial placard near Apache Spring

Camp Bowie

"The situation was by no means an enviable one. Men and officers .. worn out with fatigue .. but water we must have, and to obtain it we must force the enemy's almost impregnable position; a garrison with .. the bravest warriors of the combined Apache tribes."

Our line dashed forward, and advanced under a continuous and galling fire from both sides of the canon until we reached a point within fifty yards of the spring .. Then from the rocks and willows above the spring came a sheet of flame.

I ordered the men to fix bayonets and make one dash for the summit. The next moment we were over a rough stone wall and on the inside of a circular fortification some 30 feet in diameter; fifty or more Indians were going out and down the hill on the opposite side.

As we carried the hill a cheer came up from down below; as our comrades dashed to the spring with camp kettles and canteens, fire opened upon them from the opposite hill, but we turn a plunging fire upon the enemy, and they were soon in full flight. The howitzers were brought into action and from our elevated position we could see hundreds of Indians scampering to the hill to escape the bursting shells."

Sergeant Albert Fountain
July 15-16, 1862

closed access to the spring to all but the Apaches.

As they fled east, the Confederate force had briefly skirmished with the Apaches. On July 15, the Apaches allowed the Cavalry column in pursuit to enter the fold between the hills. The soldiers covered nearly two thirds of the distance to the spring before the Apaches opened fire. A hail of bullets descended onto the infantry and mounted troops. We can only imagine the horror of the men who suddenly came under attack, already weakened by their advance in the summer heat.

Apache Spring

Captain Rogers realized that an attempt a retreat to Dragoon Spring, and possibly Tucson, would be deadly, as many of the men would succumb to heatstroke. They must have water. Their best chance of survival was to fight for their lives. Only later did the troops learn that they were badly outnumbered, fighting 500 Apaches, led by veteran warriors. Captain Rogers pulled his men back to the entrance of the wash where he ordered his men to assemble the howitzers. Again, they advanced toward the spring.

The Cavalry's one advantage lay with the two mountain howitzers. The Apaches had built breastworks of stone on the hillside. The soldiers would later report that the bullets seem to come from behind every cactus and rock large enough to conceal a man. The infantry advanced up the wash till they reached a former stagecoach station with thick adobe walls that had been abandoned due to the Apache raids. From the station, the fire of the howitzers fell short of the Apache warriors. Captain Rogers ordered his men to take the hillside from the Apaches. His men were at a severe disadvantage as they advanced against the Apaches who held the high ground.

Years later, one of the warriors present during the battle would credit 'the wagons' for their defeat. This was the term the Apaches used for the howitzers. With their advance, the first shell broke over the hillside, killing 65 warriors and wounding many others. The fire from the Apaches began to diminish, allowing the troops to move forward in the late afternoon. At last, the troops prevailed, and reached the water they desperately needed. Throughout the night each camp could hear the other moving through the darkness.

When dawn first lightened the sky above the hills, the Apaches attempted to take back control of the spring. Their rifles made little headway against the howitzers and they disappeared into the Chiricahua Mountains. Colonel James Carleton ordered a camp to be built in the pass to spport the fight against the Chiricahua and Mesilla Apaches and to protect the vital spring. The camp is now designated as Fort Bowie National Historic Site.

Today, the spring is a trickle of water against the dark face of a rock lined with green algae. Most of the water has been diverted to a local ranch. During seasonal precipitation, the water may flow down Siphon Wash a short distance before sinking into the alluvial sands near the bottom of the hill. The riparian zone below the spring draws wildlife to the trickle of water. Damsel flies and other insects buzz over the surface. Desert brush crowds the channel following the hillside terrain.

In a time when we so easily turn on a faucet it is hard to grasp the significance of a small spring in the back country. Both the Apaches and the soldiers were dependent on the water the spring provided and were willing to fight for it.

Ownership of a spring in the early settlement of Arizona was often contentious. The legal rights to the use of most springs was established as white settlers moved into the southwest. They ignored the existing claims to the land grants by the Spanish.

The rights claimed by the early settlers were grandfathered in when Arizona developed a legal code. Springs on federal land without a legal deed showing ownership were considered to be open to public access unless a federal agency restricted their use. As townships began to form, the disputes over water for their residents sometimes led to authorities being summoned and potentially a lawsuit.

In one instance, with the Old Town Spring in Flagstaff, a night in jail seemed to temper the claim of ownership. While the railroad held the rights to Old Town spring, residents drew water from the spring for their daily usage. During dry spells, the flow from Old Town slowed to a mere trickle. A local man, Mr. Rumsey, frequently dozed beside the spring through the evening as he held a ladle to catch the the thin trickle of water. As the ladle filled, he dumped the water into a bucket and resumed his nap with the ladle back under the trickle.

He eventually decided the spring should be entirely his and proceeded to erect a fence around the spring thus preventing his neighbors from using the spring. This misdeed was reported to the local constabulary and an officer arrived to inspect the fence. Mr. Rumsey was arrested and spend the night in jail until the matter could be brought before the court. In the morning Mr. Rumsey's attitude had become more reasonable and he promised to remove the fence and pay court cost. This was one of the milder disputes over a spring.

When demand exceeded what Old Town Spring could provide, Charles Clark boasted, "There is an immense supply of water close under the surface and in 1886, when Old Town Spring went dry, I supplied Flagstaff with water, at 50 cents a barrel, which we drew from a six-foot well and which we couldn't pump dry."*

As Flagstaff continued to grow, residents came to rely on Big Leroux Spring. Barrels of water were hauled to town in a horse-drawn wagon. Residents would hang a white flag on the front of home or business, indicating their water barrels needed to be refilled. Prices started at 25 cents up to one dollar per barrel.

In a town built with pine from the surrounding forest, fire was a considerable threat. Fires were fought with bucket brigades and hand-pumps sending a thin stream from a tank mounted on a wagon. Flagstaff endured a series of fires that destroyed homes and much of the business district. By 1888, residents were calling for a water distribution system with a dependable source of water.

The Atlantic and Pacific Railroad had claimed the rights to productive springs found in the inner basin of the San Francisco Peaks near Flagstaff. Mayor Julius Aubineau approached the A&P Railroad directors and negotiated an agreement that would bring water from the springs of the inner basin to the town for thirty years at $100 a year. The city also purchased land on the west side of Flagstaff to build a large reservoir that would hold 2.5 million gallons. In return for rights to the spring, the city agreed to deliver 75,000 gallons of water per day to the railroad, totaling 27 million gallons per year. This meant that the railroad was entitled to 2.5 million gallons, the monthly capacity of the city's new reservoir. The A&P Railroad would give Flagstaff $2,500 in compensation toward the cost of the pipeline and reservoir.

As historian Platt Cline notes, this seemed like a good plan in light of the effort and cost of legal action to obtain the rights to the spring. Even as they assured Mayor Aubineau of their full cooperation, the directors of the A&P Railroad were to prove poor partners.

The pipeline and reservoir were completed in 1898 and the railroad immediately began filling tank cars with water to supply their depots along the rails. City officials awoke one morning to find that their water supply had reached a new low with the reservoir. The A&P had completely drained the reservoir overnight and little water remained for the town.

The reservoir was allowed to refill as residents carefully rationed their supplies and by Christmas 1898, the city's water system was fully operational. By 1899, the A&P had accumulated a considerable balance owed to the city for the water drawn from the pipeline and ignored invoices for the balance due until the city reduced the amount they could draw.

With a new century dawning, the town completed more work at the inner

*They Came to the Mountain, Platt Cline, Northland Publishing, 1976

Inner Basin of the San Francisco Peaks

basin springs increasing the flow of water. The city asked the Santa Fe Railroad, who had bought the A&P, to reimburse part of their expense; the directors of the railroad declined. Instead they began hauling long strings of up to 30 tank cars filled with water from the springs to their depots along the line. Once again, the unpaid invoices became delinquent. There is no record of why the rail companies did not stay current on their account but the city ordered that the Santa Fe be allowed only 50,000 gallons a day, the minimum required by their engines. The agreement had outlived the bonhomie for both parties. The railroad began pumping water from O'Neil spring, eight miles south of Flagstaff and laid claim to Sterling Spring at the junction of Pumphouse and Oak Creek Canyons.

When the city once again expanded, tapping three additional springs in the Inner Basin, the Santa Fe refused to share the cost of labor and equipment. By 1916, Judge E.M. Doe recommended that the Inner Basin be allowed to revert back to the Federal Government. The City of Flagstaff could then apply for direct access without dealing with the railroad. The directors of the Santa Fe Railroad threatened to sue. In return, the city did sue the railroad over the cost of repairs to a street crossing and the delinquent account. After a series of counter offers and accusations of delaying serious negotiations, the railroad agreed to surrender the rights to the springs and build a new reservoir with a second pipeline in exchange for a guarantee of 200,000 gallons a day. In 25 years, the city could buy the rights to the springs and sell the water to the railroad for fifteen cents per 1,000 gallons. The Flagstaff City council agreed. Work was completed by the spring of 1915 as the winter snows began to melt and sink into the cinders of the Inner Basin.

By 1938, the directors of the railroad no longer had an interest in the springs. The steam locomotives were replaced by engines powered with diesel fuel, thus ending one of the longest running fights over the water flowing from a spring within Arizona.

Today, a pipeline still carries water from the Inner Basin springs into Flagstaff's reservoirs, though the city primarily depends on deep wells that draw water from the Coconino Aquifer. In 2010, the pipeline was severely damaged when the Shultz Pass fire swept across the eastern face of the San Francisco Peaks and onto the Elden Ridge. As the embers cooled, the summer rains arrived, drenching the charred slopes with an intense downpour. Without the forest cover, the water swept down the ravines and into the community of Doney Park. The flooding destroyed roads and damaged homes. When the flooding ended, crews from the City of Flagstaff and the United States Forest Service climbed what was left of the pipeline road to survey the damage.

They found that the torrents of water had broken the pipeline where it crossed large ravines and destroyed much of the road that followed the pipeline. Large boulders had crushed the pipe beyond repair. While the springs contributed only a porion of the water required by city residents, there was no question that the city would rebuild the pipeline. First, the road had to be rebuilt. The crews spoke of their tremendous respect for the men who had laid the first line of pipe by hand. Huge machines now levered the pipe into place. Two years after the fire, water began to flow through the pipeline once again.

This was not the last battle fought over Arizona springs and a pipeline. In 1881, the town of Tombstone was running out of water. This is strange to say as flooding was becoming a problem in the depths of the mines that once supported the town. Silver had been discovered by Ed Schiefflin in the 1870s and over the next decade 25 mines had been dug around Tombstone. The Tough Nut Mine had reached a depth of 520 feet and water was beginning to seep through the rock walls into the mine shaft.

The layers of rock that rest below the town are sedimentary deposits of sandstone and limestone. Volcanic intrusions cut through the sedimentary rock to form the hills around Tombstone. As is sometimes the case with limestone, the ground water carried an unpalatable taste for human consumption. The water may have been contaminated by chemicals used in the amalgamators separating the gold from the rock ore. This meant that the water filling the mines was not a ready supply for the thirsty residents of Tombstone. The miners needed potable water and this was in short supply. *

Mine owners began looking at the Huachuca Mountains that lay 20 miles west of Tombstone. Good, clear water flowed down the canyons from springs

---

* In 1902, the Tombstone Consolidated Mining company did supply water to Tombstone for a period of time that was mixed with water from the springs.

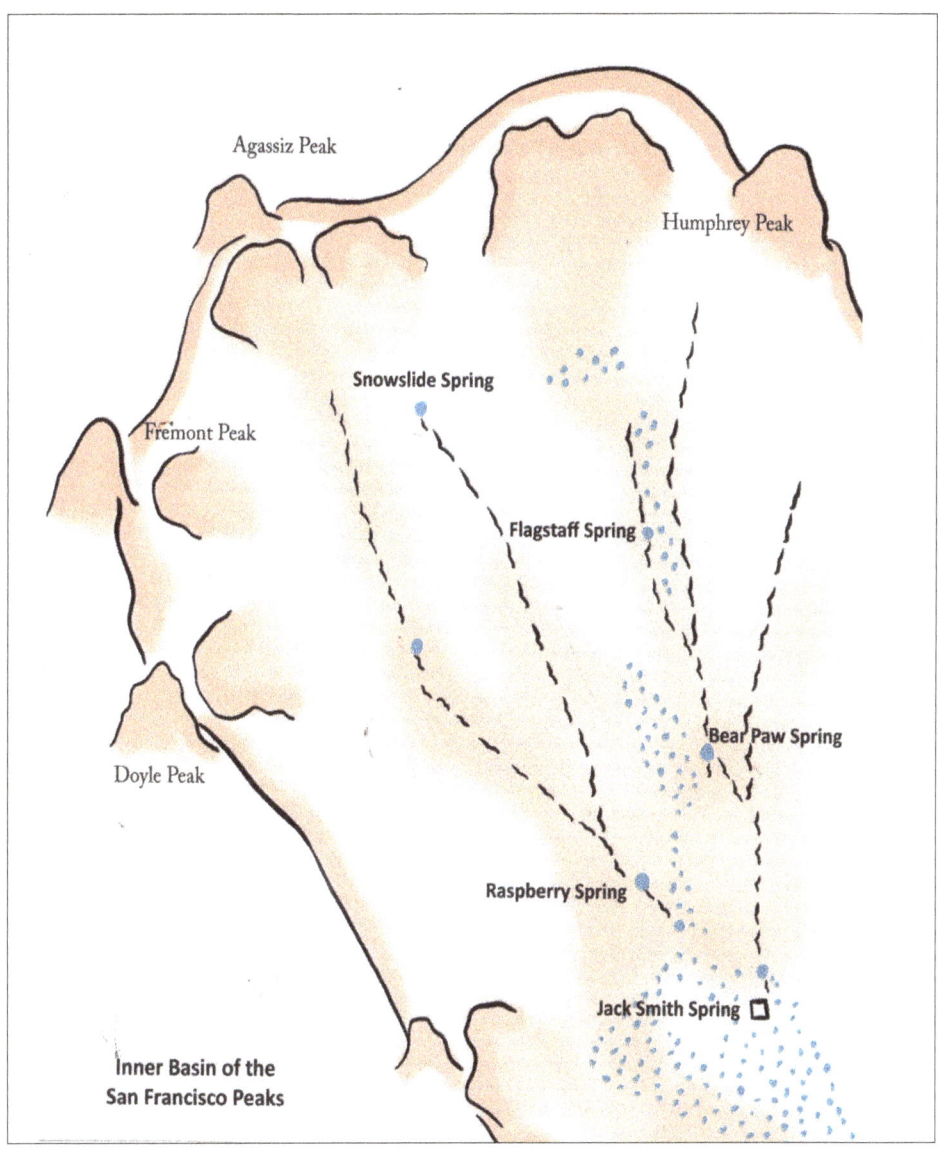

The Inner Basin of the San Francisco Peak retains 500 feet or more of alluvial and glacial deposits overlaying volcanic rock. Thirteen wells have been drilled below the springs, four in production with the remainder for observation. The Inner Basin receives on average 25-40 inches of precipitation annually, producing up to 2.5 million gallons of water a day. If not harvested within two years, the water recedes to a depth where it is unavailable.

high in the mountain range. In 1881, a crew of men climbed up Miller and Carr Canyons. The miners boasted years of experience in turning earth's resources to their advantage. Over the next few months, they dug trenches and laid a seven-inch diameter pipe over 24 miles, from the springs of Miller and Carr to the town of Tombstone. No pumps were required as the water flowed under the force of gravity alone.

In June 2011, the water still flowed through the pipeline. The original conduit had been replaced at least twice but the springs consistently provided water to Tombstone for 129 years. On June 12, the first flicker of flame burst across a hillside laden with dry brush. The Monument fire swept across the eastern exposure of the Huachucas. At night the flames glowed against the darkness as residents in Sierra Vista kept watch against the fire. One month later, July 12, the US Forest Service announced that the Monument Fire was 100% contained.

In places the pipeline channeling water from the Huachuca Mountains to Tombstone lays directly on the ground.

Two days before containment, the monsoonal flow had moved into Arizona, bringing waves of rain against the fire-blasted slopes. Concerned about potential flooding, the US Forest Service had placed rain gauges and sensors in Miller and Carr Canyon. On July 10, a microburst descended over the two canyons, dropping just over an inch and a half on the debris that littered the slopes. Of this amount, three quarters of an inch occurred within a ten-minute window.

Forest managers understand that a low-level fire will burn the underbrush but do little damage to the roots of the giant pines that retain the soil on steep slopes. However, in an upper-story fire, the flames light up the pines like matchsticks and destroy everything, leaving a moonscape that cannot hold a major deluge of rain. After an upper-story fire, there are no trees or brush to retain the soil on the steep slopes. The sensors located in Miller and Carr Canyon warned that debris was starting to slide, swept downhill by the force of the water that overwhelmed the rocks and loose soil.

In Tombstone, Mayor Jack Henderson ordered the pipeline to be shut down as the Monument Fire began moving across the face of the mountains. He did not want to see debris and fire retardant pass through the pipeline into the city's 1.2 million gallon reservoir. As the summer rains ceased, crews climbed through the debris at the mouth of Miller Canyon to inspect the damage to the pipeline. The damage was catastrophic. A wall of debris had swept down the stream with the leading edge from two feet up to seven feet high, according to the official post-fire study.

The springs that supplied the water to the pipeline had vanished under the debris. What remained of the pipeline in the upper canyon lay twisted and broken. No water would be flowing into Tombstone's reservoir. The town would now rely on city wells, one of which had a slightly higher level of arsenic than was usually found in Arizona's wells.

In most locations, city crews would clean out the debris with heavy equipment and replace the pipeline. As the equipment began rolling in, Tombstone ran into a major obstacle - the Wilderness Act of 1964. The Forest Service ordered the city to cease and desist and to remove their equipment from the canyon.

The Miller Peak Wilderness Area was established in 1984. Miller and Carr Canyons are officially designated as wilderness. The legislation forbids, not just the use, but even the presence of mechanized equipment in a wilderness area. The US Forest Service, in observance of the Act refused to allow the City of Tomb-

A thick patch of Equisetum hyemale, or scouring reeds, in a depression below a broken pipe along Miller Canyon.

stone to bring heavy equipment into Miller and Carr canyons. The City, in turn, argued that they had previously repaired damage to the pipeline after fires in 1977 and in 1983, both prior to the designation of Miller Peak. Tensions began to build between the opposing parties. At one point, even a wheelbarrow became a point of contention due to the claim that the wheel allowed mechanized motion.

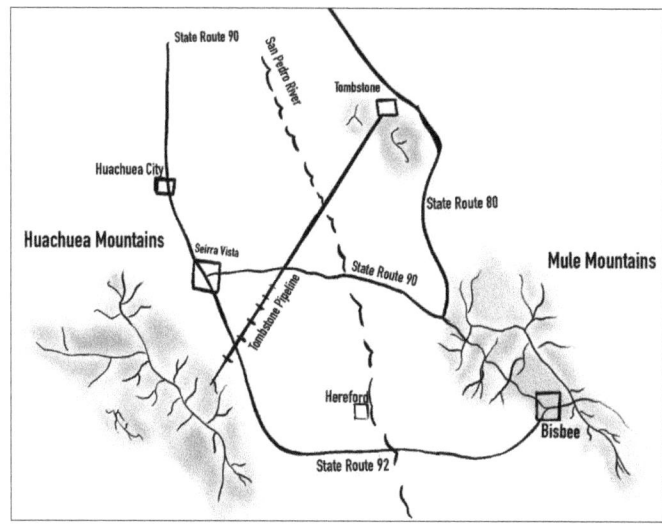

As if that were not enough, residents along the two canyons expressed concern that their homes might become construction sites if the heavy equipment was allowed to advance into the canyons. They argued that Tombstone had water from the wells and was using the damage from the fire as an opportunity to expand their pipeline. They argued that the presence of the heavy equipment would be detrimental to the canyon ecology and the wildlife that moved through the canyons.

In August 2011, Tombstone's 1.2 million gallon reservoir ran dry.

Suddenly, the issue of the town's dependence on the mountain springs, the very idea that water is life, surged to the forefront. Emotions ran high as Tombstone citizens pleaded with residents in Sierra Vista who opposed the construction and with the Forest Service to take their claims seriously. Lawyers for the opposing side argued that their claims were without due merit. In December 2011, the City of Tombstone filed a lawsuit against the US Forest Service. National news media began portraying their suit as the little guy taking on the monolithic government agency. Regardless of the legal fight, the fact remained that the US Forest Service would not allow heavy equipment on wilderness-designated land and Tombstone was running low on water. They could not sustain their current level of service on the available supply.

As I researched the springs of Arizona, I had repeatedly asked what happened to a spring after a wildfire and the debris-filled flooding that followed. Would the spring eventually re-emerge? Or would the debris on the slopes permanently bury the springs. I had witnessed what had happened with Rucker Lake in the southern reaches of the Chiricahua Mountains. Now I wondered whether the springs of Miller Canyon could restore their flow without human intervention. The City of Tombstone did not have decades to wait for the springs to re-emerge.

In the 2008, Arizona, like much of the United States, had entered a major economic recession. Across the country, men and women lost their businesses and homes as the country struggled to recover. Like many others, Kevin Rudd lost his construction business and chose to move to Tombstone with the plan to start anew. Mayor Jack Henderson, frustrated over the delay in resolving the fight with the Forest Service, asked Rudd to see if he could dig out the springs. Town archivist Nancy Sosa produced a map dating back to 1901 that showed Rudd the location of the springs in Miller Canyon.

The slopes of the Huachuca Mountains are steep with volcanic outcroppings. Climbing through a debris field increased the challenge already found in the steep ascent. Rudd found that the pipeline in Carr Canyon had remained somewhat intact and could be repaired. However, in Miller Canyon, the landmarks that would have told him where the springs had emerged had been completely wiped from the landscape within the canyon.

Miller Creek and the Tombstone pipeline.

Along with two other men, he began to probe the debris, digging through sand and rock, brush and logs. Working 10 to 12 hour days, the men sometimes dug as deep as twelve feet. Each time they uncovered a spring, they surrounded the outlet with sandbags to keep loose debris from burying the spring once again. As the springs began to flow, the water carved new channels along the streambed, increasing the volume of water flowing down the canyon.

Rudd's crew numbered from two to six men as they labored to dig trenches for a new pipeline but the challenge of bringing new pipe up the canyon remained. The State of Arizona has a prison near the town of Douglas, twenty-five miles from the Huachucas. Tombstone turned to the inmates at the prison to assist their efforts. The prison has several crews that can be found working on projects along the road of southern Arizona. Strictly on a volunteer basis, the prisoners stepped up to the challenge of moving the pipe ten miles up the steep slopes by carrying the pipe on their shoulders. Some helped dig the trenches using shovels and picks. Along portions of the route, the pipe was simply laid on top of the ground.

Six years later, when we climbed the canyon, I found the vegetation had restored the natural appearance of a canyon altered by the flooding that had occurred in 2011. Along the streambed, water seeped from fractured rocks, increasing the volume with every half mile. Descending into the streambed, we found sections of old pipe that no longer carried the water to Tombstone's reservoir. The oldest is a dark iron, pitted from years of exposure. To one who knows standard pipe sizes, this is a relic. The pipe is seven inches in diameter, no longer a standard size. The thick collars connecting each section were originally fitted on site. Running our hands along this relic, we were in awe of the men who persevered in building the first pipeline with nothing but hand tools to carry water over 24 miles.

Other pipe appears, both dark grey and white plastic or nylon. One broken end hangs over the edge of an embankment, speaking of the natural forces that tore the pipe apart. The water trickles into a depression filled with scouring reeds.

The lawsuit between Tombstone and the US Forest Service came to a final ruling. Tombstone had argued that their claim to the springs lay in agreements formed in the 1800s. Nancy Sosa's cache of old agreements and deeds became the basis upon which the claims were settled. While Tombstone laid claim to 24 springs, the judge ultimately ruled that the city had a legitimate claim to two springs in Miller, two springs in Carr, and to Clark Spring, located between the two canyons. In the ruling, the city made little progress against the force of the Wilderness Act of 1964. The judge ruled they could lay claim to a fifty-foot corridor along the pipeline, based on vested property rights and a special use permit in 1962, but the Wilderness Act remained in effect. Any future repairs will once again depend on the shoulders and backs of men skilled in the use of third-class levers and the ability to climb steep slopes.

The case will undoubtably be cited in future lawsuits over the use of springs and rights of private property owners. When asked what was more valuable, the life of a spotted owl or the life of a human, the judge could not move beyond the law. Most would argue that human life cannot give way to the rights of a spotted owl. Yet, this has become a point of contention repeatedly in lawsuits throughout the west.

Another case where opposing interests are creating a a conflict that has landed in the courts is found in the Santa Rita Mountains. In 2007, the parent company of Rosemont Mine filed a proposed plan for an open air copper mine in the foothills of the Santa Rita Mountains. Five years later as the Coronado Forest Service prepared to release the final Environmental Impact Statement, a storm of protest descended over the proposal.

The mine would have provided a number of good paying jobs, however, environmentalists are concerned the cost to the ecosystems of the Santa Ritas might be devastating. As I talked with officials in Pima County, I could see cause for concern. This huge operation would have spread over 4,755 acres, three quarters of which would have been Forest Service land. The impact statement dealt with the impact to air quality and both ground and surface water. Some of the concern regarding water:

- As huge mining buckets bite into the layers of rock, sedimentary rock would have been exposed, potentially allowing water to drain from the aquifer into an open pit. The EIS suggested that up to 31 % of the aquifer could be lost, much of this to evaporation. Estimates of the loss total 170 to 370 acre feet of water per year depending on the model used.

- Of 132 springs, 63 would be lost, along with their riparian habitat.

- The pit would leave a huge pond of contaminated water which would leach into the ground and potentially reach the aquifer. The EPA questioned whether the leaching would perform as expected, removing both solids and chemicals. The study models may not have been applicable to our region.

- Huge deposits of rock would be left in massive ridges on forest service land. As precipitation fell on this rock, it would run off into neighboring creeks, potentially contaminating the surface water. As the rock tailings hardened under the sun, little vegetation would grow. Without vegetation, run-off would cause flooding.

Geohydrologists would be the first to tell you they do not completely understand the channels that water follows through layers of rock. The Santa Ritas are a range with lush vegetation. Many of the canyons are an oasis for the wildlife, as well as the people seeking refuge from modern life. If we begin to strip the water from this range, we do not know how the range as a whole will be affected. And no one will be watching.

In 2019, Judge James Soto overturned the mine's operating permit issued by the Forest Service, creating a whole new storm of protests.

In his objections, Jared Blumenfeld, with the Environmental Protection Agency, noted that the modeling done for the EIS was not in line with the environment found in the Santa Rita Mountains. This modeling could obviously skew the results of the operation as it proceeded. For instance, the modeling of rainwater leaching through the rock waste into the ground was based on a steady, light rain rather than the torrential microburst that occur in the southwest.

Judge Soto's ruling halts development of the mine until these concerns as well as those effecting air quality can be addressed. No further progress on the mine is expected until 2023.

Another battle is brewing in the basin at the foot of the Huachuca Mountain. Subdivisions of tract homes are rapidly being built in the San Pedro River plain. Local residents ask where the water is coming from to support the people who live in these homes. In other communities across southern Arizona, water is being pumped from aquifers at a rate that cannot be sustained. When conservationists protest against the draining of the aquifers, residents are quick to question their compassion for the people who live in these areas.

"We can't live without water!"

There is no official discussion of capping the subdivisions that are being built in this arid region. Even as more building permits are issued, officials shrug and say, "This corporation has a right to develop the land they own."

Many conservative residents of the western states are all for small government and less interference in their lives. However, a lack of water would severely inhibit the lives of those who already live in this arid climate. This may be one issue which requires that we limit our growth to better manage the resources we have been given.

Like the myth of the Old West where gunfights might break out over the use of a spring or water hole, tensions are rising as drought takes a toll and population numbers continue to rise. In the fight over the springs of Miller Canyon, the war of words and legal maneuvering destroyed long term relationships. No guns were pulled, no shots fired. The battle over the Tombstone pipeline should serve as a warning to begin comprehensive and common sense revision of the rights under our water laws before tensions elsewhere escalate into violence.

Preservation

In the spring of 2019, we parked at the base of the Dragoon Mountains and began to follow a dirt track rising steadily upward toward a prominent peak. Green grass spread across the sloping hillside, well-watered after a wet winter. We wove our way along the rocky track, side-stepping sharp rocks as steep hillsides rose on either side of the canyon. After a half mile, the track dropped into the floor of a wash. We turned to follow the boulder-choked drainage seeking a historic spring that had given water to travelers over the previous three centuries.

In the past, water seeped from the earth to pool in the low spots along the wash. Native Americans had bent to fill their skin bags and hand-sculpted pots. Cavalry officers directed troops to bring their mounts for a long thirst-quenching drink from the cool water. Stage coach passengers eagerly wet their dusty faces with water channeled to the coach station. And in time, cattlemen brought cattle to the pastures below the spring. The water of Dragoon Spring sustained the lives of those who used it for over three hundred years.

We faced a dry creek bed, peering upstream and down, wondering which direction we should turn. I searched for a cottonwood that would mark the presence of water near the surface but found only gambrel oak and mountain mahogany pushing their way skyward. We scrambled upward through each bend in the wash expecting some sign of water. Only dry sand and rock met us at every turn. Finally admitting defeat, we turned back and there a few yards down the wash stood a mortared rock wall jutting from the hillside. How had we missed that on our ascent?

Eagerly, I peered around the edge of the wall to find dry sand abutting the wall of the wash. Not one damp grain appeared as witness of what had once been a historic spring. Disappointed, I contemplated the history of Dragoon Spring and the changes that have occurred over the last one hundred years. In the last five centuries, records show us this state has passed through droughts and years of good rainfall. We currently see our land caught in a climatic change that has brought an ever drier landscape.

As I looked around the dry wash, I acknowledged that Dragoon Spring is one more point of deprivation brought on by overuse and drought. I had not failed to notice the lengths of black nylon pipe cast aside by crews that had channeled the water down to the rusting stock tanks. I wondered if all the flow had been diverted or if the aquifer was dropping as pumps pulled water skyward from the wells that supported a local community.

As with many hillside springs, pools of water along the wash once created a riparian environment nurturing the native plants and animals living in the Dragoons. When the water ceased to flow, the riparian zone dried out. Plants died, wildlife, insects and birds ceased coming to what was a perennial source of water. Staring at the hillside behind the wall, I tried to detect where the water might have emerged. A trickle might return after a sufficient snowfall but it seemed unlikely that the riparian zone could once again thrive within this desert wash.

This was not the only spring we encountered that showed signs of depletion. The cattle industry has diverted water from

De-watered Dragoon Spring

many of the state's larger springs to raise steak on the hoof for a meat-hungry population. Further north, buffalo first introduced into the grasslands of House Rock Valley have now entered the Grand Canyon National Park and turned springs into mud wallows. This was not foreseen by the original investors in a scheme to provide buffalo for avid hunters.

Other springs have been devastated by all-terrain vehicles. Many urban dwellers will motor past such a site and wonder at the concern over a depleted spring. *Yes, it is sad,* they would reason, *but I can turn a faucet handle in my kitchen for a drink. The spring is gone.* And with a momentary glance they turn to other concerns.

Not so fast! Take a moment to think beyond the immediate absence of a spring. What does the absence of water say about the world around us? Is this a natural event possibly due to drought or the shifting of the earth beneath our feet? Or do we bear some responsibility for the depletion?

It is easy to shrug and move on. After all, most of us are not trained geohydrologists. But this is a question that is worth considering. I talked with Jeri Ledbetter, the director for the Springs Institute about the threats to Arizona's springs.

Considering my question, she stared out the window for a moment, then said, "We tend to call the springs the canary's canary."

In the 1800s, men tunneled deep underground following the veins of coal that interlaced the Appalachian Mountains. As they worked, they kept a small canary in a bird cage where the miners could see and hear the bird. If the bird toppled over, the miners knew that poisonous gas had leaked into the mine and they in turn were endangered.

Jeri is saying that the springs serve as a warning that the aquifers deep underground are being drawn down faster than can be replenished. We have not cared for the environment in a way that encourages the wild lands to thrive and be preserved for future generations.

Public discussions regarding drought and how our water resources are allocated warn us this resource must be conserved and managed well. The springs, quiet and unassuming, have become the canary reminding us that not all is well with this natural resource.

Within Arizona, two organizations work with land managers across the state to restore and preserve the springs: in southern Arizona, the Sky Island Alliance and in northern Arizona, the Springs Institute of the Museum of Northern Arizona. In the next few pages we'll look at some of the work done by these organizations as well as other efforts to protect, to preserve or at least mitigate the damage being done to the springs and to the aquifers collecting water deep underground.

Hoxworth is a small rheocrene spring that appears in a wash southwest of Lake Mary near Flagstaff. At one time, the spring's flow may have followed a wash to Lake Mary. Today, the water dissipates into the years of sediment that have accumulated along its course. Wells drilled by homeowners in the area have tapped the shallow aquifer that lies beneath the ridge of this watershed, though some choose to haul water for their personal use.

Beginning in the late 1800s cattle and sheep were driven onto the Colorado Plateau to graze among the pines. Hoxworth Spring would have been a valuable watering hole for the livestock. Along with the cattle came logging men who dropped huge ponderosa pines to feed the demand for timber from the railroad. Much of the timber was hauled to the mills by trains that ran along rails laid over

Pool at Hoxworth Spring

square beams. Hoxworth would have provided some water, particularly in the early months of the year, to the locomotives that pulled these trains. Both industries would have men and animals moving over the loose earth that bordered the spring and wash, steadily packing down the soil. The packed soil would have allowed the snow and rain to run off much more quickly than if healthy ground cover absorbed the moisture. As season followed season, the natural course of the spring began to alter with runoff shaping the walls of the watercourse.

As our nation moved into the 1900s, a rising conservation movement began to raise awareness toward preserving what remained of the vast forests that had once carpeted much of our continent. Much of the forest that covered the eastern states was gone. As the timber industry moved into the western states, conservationists realized that the arid west could not easily reproduce the native forests with the limited amount of rainfall. Many of the stream beds were eroding as the denuded hillsides no longer held back the water. Sheep and cattle trampled river banks and springs, tearing up the soft ground with sharp, heavy hooves. Where once clear springs of water had flowed, clay-laden muck and tainted pockets of water remained.

In 1905, President Theodore Roosevelt signed legislation that created the US Forest Service with a mission to protect the wild lands remaining in the western states. When the Great Depression hit the country in the 1930s, President Franklin D. Roosevelt instigated legislation creating the Civilian Conservation Corps as part of the new Public Works Administration. Crews of men streamed out across the west building roads and national parks. Part of their efforts were aimed at restoring creek beds and badly damaged springs. These efforts became a blueprint for future conservation but they did not protect the springs from future misuse.

Landowners still diverted the springs and ranchers did not always protect the springs from their cattle. Hot springs were channeled into pools for those afflicted with physical ailments. As recently as the 1980s, the Environmental Protection Agency began to place regulations on springs, which, in spite of the agency's good intentions, withheld water from some of the species that depended on the springs for survival.

When Dr. Abe Springer, a geohydrologist, first came to Hoxworth Spring, he found the banks along the watercourse deeply cut and eroded. In places the bank stood nearly five feet tall. Clumps of grass clung to the floor of the wash separated by riven fingers of bare earth. The vertical banks would allow water to race down the wash without settling into the earth. Without a defined watercourse, in time, the collection of sediment would elimate any aquatic species depending on the spring.

When a spring is considered for restoration, a survey is first done for the area around the spring. At Hoxworth Spring, Dr. Springer's students, along with the staff of the Springs Institute, divided the riparian zone into plats, which are further divided into smaller sections. Taking one section at a time, they list each species of vegetation found in a section along with the condition of the soil, and whether water is present, either standing or just beneath surface.

Imagine stooping for hours, sometimes in mud, clutching a pencil and pad, counting and sketching. In cool weather, one's fingers ache from the cold. In warm temperatures, the mind slows as the body heats up and sweat rolls down one's face. Not only are the plants innumerated, but small inverbrate creatures are added to the count. Prints of animals visiting the area are logged, causing mild excitement. After all, who wouldn't pause to glance around after spotting a four-inch wide print of a large cat.

Once the survey is completed, the information is compiled. The team studies historical records on the springs and the contours of the land. A plan is drawn up to sculpt the terrain into a more natural flow.

At Hoxworth Spring, as with Pakoon Spring on the Arizona Strip, heavy equipment was brought in by trailer. The blades bit into the eroded banks, creating a gently sloped streambed. Erosion mats, made from natural and synthetic material, were placed along

the stream's course. Species of carex were planted and seed for grass and wildflowers broadcast across the loose dirt. Hydromulching protected the seed. A fence was erected around the spring and along the watercourse below the outlet. The fence was intended to keep cattle, elk and deer, along with four-wheeled vehicles, out of the streambed. No mud bogging was going to uproot restoration efforts.

I'm always a bit disappointed to walk up on a fence surrounding a restored streambed. Water calls me and I want to step up to the pools and dabble my fingers through the clear stream. In warm weather, I long to wade in a pool to cool my tired feet. Such activity that seems so harmless may actually bring the first deterioration to the fragile ecosystem of the spring.

I did question whether the fence would deter wildlife from reaching the water. Upon further consideration, smaller animals could creep through the fence. The larger ungulates can easily stride to the area below the fenced portion and find small pools of water to quench their thirst. The fence allows the riparian area to become well-established before the sharp hooves begin to tear at the vegetation surrounding the spring.

Researchers have found that reducing the number of trees and vegetation around the spring helps to increase the flow of water. Once removed, the roots of larger species are no longer absorbing the water before it reaches the surface.

As the restoration efforts drew to a close, Dr. Springer felt a sense of accomplishment. Several years later he found a road had been ripped the length of the valley on the hillside above the spring to serve the logging trucks hauling massive ponderosa pines to the mill. Returning home, he called the Forest Service to ask just what they were thinking after all the work done to restore the spring. Why had a permit been issued to the logging company for this road? As with much restoration work in the back country, one effort to conserve may be at cross purposes with another program. On a positive note, the logging would reduce the number of trees drawing water from the soil which in turn would increase the outflow of the spring.

In May of 2018, I dropped into the watershed above Griffith Spring to photograph how the flow of a rivulet of snowmelt is measured with a small water weir. In the soft mud, the prints of deer and elk held water that had seeped into the depressions from the inundated soil. Along the small stream, the grass had grown tall, easily 12-14 inches high. The grass lay in thick swathes for yards on either wide of the stream. This thick layer protects the soil along the banks.

General Spring lies on the edge of the Mogollon Rim and has undergone rehabilitation. The cabin at General Spring has been completely restored. Hikers along the Arizona Trail frequently stop by to peer in the windows and read the small sign. The cabin dates back to 1915 when it was completed by Louis Fisher as a fire watch cabin for the Forest Service. Rangers used the cabin as a base while patrolling the forests along the rim. The cabin remained in service into the 1960s and was restored in 1989 as a historical site.

Wet meadow

In front of the cabin, we found a dry meadow covered with clump grass in need of moisture. Along one edge of the meadow was a shallow wash carpeted with grass nearly waist-high. The grass was a deep green, the tips laden with seed. Parting the grass to make our way across the bottom of the wash, the ground felt spongy. I stooped to take a closer look and found the soil not just damp but wet. No surprise that the grass grew so well. I could imagine the elk standing in the lush grass filling their bellies. This is a hypocrene spring, the water released through transpiration.

Turning back to the cabin, near the edge of the wash, we found a shallow well, the bottom bone dry. At one time the perched aquifer may have welled up to fill the rock-lined well with water for the cabin's residents. Nearby we found a cement pad with a cap over the entrance of a small cistern.

Looking at the heavy cover of grass, the healthy riparian zone is obvious to the casual visitor. Runoff descending from the hillside, is first

Dry well

absorbed by the soil which in turn supports the growth of the grass. As the runoff increases the tall grass slows the flow of the water as it passes along the channel. The grass protects the soil from the hooves of large mammals that may venture into the wash.

Further downstream, the Arizona Trail passes through the riparian zone. The wash has been fenced against the destructive nature of human traffic. Undoubtably, hikers passing along the trail found this a lovely stretch for camping and soon the vegetation was worn to bare dirt, the stream banks beginning to erode, cut by spring runoff. The fence has allowed the riparian zone to recover and once again vegetation covers the banks of the stream along the canyon. A small hillside spring has reached the surface to trickle along the watercourse.

Not every spring can be restored. The resources are limited and the volunteers willing to put in long hours of tedious effort are few. However, restoration is only part of the effort to preserve Arizona's springs.

The second part of preserving our springs lies in responding to the threat to our aquifers. In May 2018, Julia Fonseca led me toward three displays in the Pima County Office for Sustainability. The first was a photo of the early farming efforts on the Santa Cruz River, using irrigation ditches. Then, she led me to a diagram of the plot map for the families farming along the Santa Cruz. And finally a map that is one of the oldest maps of the southwest and northern Mexico.

Research by archeologists show that Spanish settlers adapted the irrigation ditches of the Hohokam to farm along the Santa Cruz. In this display, I could see hands-on evidence of the fields that were used to produce the grains and farm produce that once fed both ancient people and the Spanish that first settled in this territory.

During an excavation a couple of decades back, a heavy equipment operator was using a backhoe to assist an archeological dig when he noticed an irregularity in the soil texture. He stepped off the machine to check the hole before calling over the archeologist. He had uncovered a 4,000 year old field with evidence of the people who had lived and worked there: the corn planting holes, the footprints of the farmer, the knee and hand prints of a child falling into mud, a dog running across the site. all left in mud that had dried and been covered by coarse gravel.

What is so remarkable about a corn field? Here is evidence of the ordinary life of a person who lived 4,000 years ago. Nothing spectacular, just a man planting corn. He pushes his stick 18 inches into the soil and inserts a tiny kernel of seed corn. And then, he waits for the rain.

As word of the discovery became public, members of the Tohono O'odham tribe visited the site. They were very excited, certain this was evidence of the Hohokam, a people they claim as their early ancestors.

Imagine for a moment how these people lived. They had no faucets with water emerging in a steady stream of water at the flick of a wrist against a handle. The early residents along the Santa Cruz depended on surface water. They dug canals and placed a series of head gates to direct water into a succession of fields. For everyday use, the family would shoulder large *ollas,* or pots, and walk to the river to bring back the water for the day. Every drop was precious. There was no standing under a stream of water for twenty minutes in a shower or allowing the water to run as we wait for a flame of gas to heat the stream of water.

As we wandered through a conversation about the threat to the aquifers, I asked Julia what she considered the biggest threat to the aquifers in our state. Without a pause, she replied, "The internal combustion engine."

That was it. Period. Nothing more. She waited silently as I considered her answer: The internal combustion engine, the driving force within our machines, within our pumps. The internal combustion engine powers the drill rig that digs a well down through the layers of rock to a loosely packed strata where water lies along the fractures in the rock. As the water is released, a pump with an internal combustion engine brings the water to the surface. The pump can pour forth a stream of water beyond the imagination of the native man stooped over a seep dripping from a crack in a rock face.

Now we have water exploding across the surface, into tanks, along pipelines, providing us with a steady stream of cool, clear refreshment. This water did not accumulate in such a massive stream but rather drop by drop. Recently, in a meeting of the Coconino Plateau Water Advisory Council, one of the participants spoke of tests done on water emerging from a basin and range aquifer in southern Arizona. The tests revealed, he said, that the water was 40,000 years old. Furthermore, he was quite certain that any water pumped from this aquifer would not be replaced in his lifetime.

Think for a moment about the drought that has affected our state for the last two decades. We have seen rivers drop to a small percentage of what once filled their stream beds. Lake Powell and Lake Mead have dropped to their lowest levels, and water managers are now saying the river cannot sustain the withdrawals allowed under the original water pact.

In 2018, the federal government declared that the state had received sufficient snow and rainfall during the winter to remove most of our state from drought status. In the summer of 2019, the northern part of the state saw only two or three storms days with significant rainfall from the summer rains. Once again, the soil and our forests baked under the summer heat. The drought that we hoped had receded now returned with a vengeance.

Arizona uses around 2.2 trillion acre feet of water each year. The water we depend on comes from three sources. Thirty-six percent of our water is drawn from the Colorado River. Another 21 percent is taken from in-state rivers and lakes. Ground water, meaning the water pumped from our aquifers, makes up 40 percent while reclaimed water is now responsible for three percent of our water use. After doing the math, this means we are drawing 880 billion gallons out of our aquifers each year.

This is the challenge we face as Arizona, an arid land by any measure, relies heavily on the water that slides into deep wells and is pumped to the surface. This is water that has accumulated over the eons in the Coconino, the Red Wall and the Navajo aquifers along with the aquifers under the Basin and Range territory. Rainfall and the winter's snowpack replenish the aquifers but we are now using more water than replenishment can provide. The result is that our aquifers are steadily dropping.

The numbers on how we use our water are also worth contemplating. Of the 2.2 trillion gallons, 70 percent goes to agriculture, meaning fields of grain, cotton and farm crops, along with orchards and vineyards. Agriculture also includes the raising of livestock, whether in feedlots or water brought to tanks on the open range. Another five percent supports our industrial sector while around 20 percent is used for municipal requirements. Our showers, teeth brushing, cooking and water-sucking lawns fall within that 20 percent.

The good news is that Arizona residents as a whole are very conscious of water conservation. Today, we use about the same amount of water that we consumed in 1958 even though our population has exploded. This is in part due to the drop in agriculture as many of the fields near our urban centers have been developed for other uses. The stable use can also be credited to other water saving practices such as the implementation of water saving and low-flow devices. In Phoenix, many homeowners have switched to desert

> The 1980 Water Code requires a developer of a new subdivision to show they can provide a secondary source of water in addition to the primary source of water.

landscaping from the water-thirsty grass. Compared to 80 percent of homes in 1978, only 14 percent of homes now have grass covering their open space. Likewise, in agriculture, farmers have learned to cycle their crops to take advantage of seasonal cycles and modify irrigation methods, using less water.

However, despite our efforts to conserve our water resources, the fact remains that we are using more water than we receive. Just like a bank account where the withdrawals exceed the deposits, we have overdrawn our account.

Not only have we overdrawn our account but the rocks that form our aquifers are now threatened as well. Once the water is withdrawn, the fractures forming the aquifers may close up. Even if years of wet summers and winters return, the water percolating into the soil beneath our feet may not be able to restore the aquifers. In California the problem is more severe and geologists point to large cracks forming in the earth where the ground has subsided as the aquifers have declined.

In thinking about how we use water, we must examine our priorities. How are we using our water and what is the best use for the water available to us? Two recent proposals came before the Coconino Plateau Water Advisory Council for new hydroelectric plants. Each would require vast amounts of either ground or surface water to create hydroelectric power. Undoubtably, the need for electric power is great, but do we squander our ground water to provide electrical power when other alternatives might supply what is needed?

Across the Valley of the Sun in the greater Phoenix metropolitan area, we see farmland disappearing under thousands of acres of cement and asphalt. At one time, the valley was considered to be a mecca for agriculture due to the number of days of sunlight, relatively good soil and water supplied by the Salt and Gila Rivers. With low population numbers, farmers followed the example of the ancient Hohokam in building canals and flooding their fields with irrigation water. In recent years, farmers have reconsidered this practice, in part due to the the build-up of salt in the soil.

Do we want to continue to reduce the number of acreage devoted to large scale agriculture? Conservationists are beginning to question the wisdom of shipping food cross country rather than growing what we eat locally. As mentioned above, agriculture consumes a lot of water, so what is the better use of the desert surrounding metropolitan Phoenix?

One of the greater concerns for conservationists is the preservation of riparian zones along our rivers and streams. Visitors to the back country love to catch a glimpse of a massive elk among the pines or a secretive badger rippling over the surface of a dirt track. From the small water strider to the bull elk with a full rack, these animals depend on large tracts of forest and perennial sources of water to survive. Caught in the complicated routines of our lives, we may not give a thought to the water strider, but we still need the wild country and the creatures that dwell in our forests and deserts. We need the undisturbed land to maintain the towns and cities that emerge from this arid region.

In northern Arizona, two of the most contested water topics revolve around the use of reclaimed water for making snow for the Arizona Snowbowl and whether the dams across the Colorado River should be decommissioned. The first of these has resulted in public demonstrations before the Flagstaff City Council and in front of the entrance to the Snowbowl. Such discussions add a lively element to everyday routine as native people charge that their historic land and places of worship are being desecrated.

How do we set priorities for our water use? Whose voice rings louder than others? I am certain that the slow trickle of a spring is lost in the clamor over water use.

Conservation Writ Large and Small

The efforts to conserve our water resources seem to fall into two categories: The quotidian activities and those avtivities that are pro-active, requiring us to take action beyond the practice of routine conservation.

Public campaigns have called attention to conservation practices like turning off the water when brushing one's teeth. As a teenager, I loved long showers. With the birth of our children, this practice was challenged as I applied shampoo, hoping the baby would sleep just a couple more minutes. Take a moment with your next shower to time how long the water actually runs. HomeWaterWorks.org estimates that the average shower lasts eight minutes and consumes 17 gallons of water at an average flow rate of two gallons a minute. Standing under that wonderful flow of warm water, eight minutes flies by. In terms of the quantity of water used, showers come right after the toilet and the washing machine.

Then, there are dirty dishes to wash, the house to clean, cooking edible meals - all of these tasks require water. Through conservation, we can cut a minute or two off our showers, do full loads of laundry and cut our water use in meal preparation. Don't believe me? Talk to one of the men or women who live off the grid. They haul every drop of water they use and many live on less than 50 gallons of water per individual each and every week.

In talking with individuals who haul their own water, we hear them frequently describe their efforts to use each gallon at least twice. Usually this means that they take the water from household tasks such as showers or laundry and use it on landscaping or gardens. The state of Arizona allows residents to recycle this *gray water*, though the process can be challenging unless special equipment is installed when a home is built.

One of the most profitable ways to reduce water use is to collect the water that runs off our roofs during a rainstorm or from snowmelt. Water collection is very popular in other countries with arid climates. Most people are not aware that a half inch of rain on the average home, when collected in rain barrels, can produce nearly 1,000 gallons. With water saving irrigation techniques, a 1,000 gallons can go a long way in maintaining a landscape with plants that do not require much water. In desert climates, many homeowners have elected to go with rock over grass in their yards. Phoenix and Tucson have seen water usage maintaing residential lawns drop drop significantly as developers are landscaping with rock, desert plants and artificial turf.

However, our aquifers benefit when we reduce the amount of impervious surfaces within our city. This means less ground covered with cement and asphalt. Rain is allowed to soak into the soil rather than run off impervious surfaces. I understand that the city of Tucson has incorporated an infrastructure design to assist green landscapes. Some neighborhoods have introduced curb cuts that allow the water flowing in the gutters to enter property, bringing water to the landscaping much as the old fashion irrigation technique of flooding a lawn once did.

Tucson also has massive washes that run through the city and are free of development. These corridors allow water to run off the neighboring Santa Catalina Mountains, passing through the city neighborhoods to disperse across the plains at the foot of the range. The water sinks into the desert grit and into the aquifer. As a passive means of conservation, green belts can help feed our aquifers as well as reduce the stress of so many people living in close proximity.

The City of Phoenix has recycled nearly 100 percent of their effluent for years, including the water used at the Palo Verde Nuclear Plant. As the quality of reclaimed water improves with new technology, reclaimed water plays an ever more important role in the large communities built in this arid land. Recycling

Sedona Wetlands

The 'Big Guns'

effluent reduces the draw on our aquifers.

The City of Sedona is built along Oak Creek, a major tributary to the Verde River and a recreational delight to the city's residents. Standing in downtown Sedona, one might look up at the massive sandstone cliffs surrounding the town and realize that the terrain plays an important part in how this city provides water and disposes of the effluent from its residents.

The layers of sandstone above the town are water keepers. On the surface however, a violent rainstorm can send torrents of water cascading from the rock cliffs into the streets and channels below. By the same measure, finding a safe means to recycle effluent is a challenge in a land with massive rock ledges and buttes.

Along US89A, there was a shallow wash that received runoff from a large ridge on the southern edge of Sedona. Shallow pools of water often remained for several days after heavy precipitation. The city chose to develop wetlands at this site, with the effluent allowed to soak into the subterranean soils at a measured pace.

Before the effluent is released, the raw sewage passes through six steps to purify the water. A pipeline brings the raw sewage to the plant where it is filtered to remove solid waste. As the water enters an aeration basin, micro-organisms are introduced to break down the waste. The next two steps remove any remaining solids. The water then passes along a channel where it is exposed to high intensity ultraviolet rays, killing any bacteria. The water that emerges is rated A+.

This is an acceptable level for the open water ponds and the wildlife that come into the area. Today, motorists catch glimpses of open pools of water lined with a heavy growth of cattails. The ponds spreading over 27 acres are popular with ducks and mud hens. A picnic area has been developed north of the ponds. The wetlands provide homes for waterfowl as well as a network of recreational trails for residents.

The drawback is that the wetlands cannot contain all the effluent and water exposed to the hot sun allows a high rate of evaporation. Sedona set aside nearly 300 acres at the wetlands to remain under irrigation as part of their conservation efforts. Both low level sprinklers and high pressure valves distribute water over the fields. Motorists along US 89A can witness the arcs of water from the 'big guns' soaring over the treetops.

The problem with this method comes with cooler temperatures in the winter. The rate of evaporation slows and the pipes may freeze during the winter months. So, the city stops irrigating and the effluent is held in a large reservoir until spring when the temperature begins to climb.

Another issue with irrigating is the salt that begins to accumulate in the soil under irrigation. This is not uncommon but management would prefer not to have the acreage become a desert of highly mineralized soil. Sedona is surrounded

An injection well

by federally owned land which cannot be easily sold to the city for development as people flock to this beautiful region. The land used for the wetlands may be private but is no longer available for development. A committee of city staff and local citizens began to discuss how the city might recycle their effluent to benefit Sedona. A number of ideas were considered but the discussion kept returning to the idea of injecting the waste water back into the earth where it would percolate down to the aquifer.

In recent years the idea of injecting wells has become more popular. Much like a well drilled for water, the injection wells sink deep below the earth's surface. The effluent is injected into the ground where it percolates through the rock layers.

One concern arose over whether the waste would contaminate our water supply. Then again, local wildlife have left waste across the landscape for centuries. Committee members were assured that the rock layers act as a filter, removing contaminants before the effluent reaches the aquifer. Committee members visited other cities using a range of recycling methods and studied reports about the success or failure of such efforts. An injection well began to be viewed in a favorable light by the committee.

To learn whether such an effort would have a chance of being successful, city staff hired a firm to ultrasonically map the region south of the city using a process known as Controlled-source Audio-frequency Magnetotellurics (CSAMT). According to Zonge International, the process "involves transmitting a controlled electric signal at a suite of frequencies into the ground from one location (transmitter site) and measuring the received electric and magnetic fields in the area of interest (receiver site)." The signals penetrate the ground up to a 1,000 meter depth and signals received can provide a map showing any large cavities within the layers of rock.

Just as rain and snow-melt have carved the red sandstone cliffs of Sedona, so water with acidic elements has been at work underground. Precipitation has dissolved the silica and calcium carbonate found between the grains in the sandstone, creating channels and caverns underground. Sedona has at least 5 large sinkholes. At one time these were underground caverns that collapsed, dropping the surface of the earth into a deep depression.

As the ultrasonic mapping began, small black voids began to appear among the rock layers. The small black dots grew larger, indicating large caverns. It seems the ground beneath our feet is not quite so solid. City staff was informed that the rock layers looked very promising for drilling injection wells.

In their first attempt, the drill bit sank toward a large black void that had been discovered beneath the wetlands. Five hundred gallons of effluent were injected along the shaft. The water disappeared. The crew sent down a small camera to check the level of the water.

Nothing!

The water really had disappeared. The void under the wetland lay along a channel that passed through the layers of rock as a stream would pass at our feet. There would be no problem with releasing the water into the injection wells to be filtered through the rock layers into the C-aquifer. A second well has now been drilled to a depth of 1,000 feet. Each well is outfitted with a back flow chamber to manage the surge of water that bubbles upward when large amounts are injected into the narrow shaft.

Recently, Roxanne Holland, the Director for Waste Water Management, reported that the injection well has been so successful that the city has been able to retrieve 200 acres from irrigation that may now be developed for other uses. With Sedona's success, the City of Flagstaff, is now looking at injection wells to supplement their water treatment plants and wetlands.

Phoenix and its surrounding cities, are on a much a much larger scale than Sedona. The City of Phoenix relies on surface water, with ground water supplying only three per cent of what is required. Cynthia Campbell compares their aquifers to a savings deposit in the bank, held in reserve for the day when surface water may no longer meets the needs of the population

The City of Phoenix by contract uses water from the Salt River Project for specific areas in the Roosevelt Irrigation District. The Central Arizona Project supplies the remainder of the water required. But what happens to the effluent?

Unlike the small city of Sedona, there are no rock caverns under the desert grit. The City has three ways to recycle 100 percent of their effluent. Tres Rios is the largest wetlands in the state, located near the confluence of the Gila and Salt Rivers. Another portion of the effluent is sent to the Palo Verde Nuclear Plant and used repeatedly before the water is allowed to evaporate in large holding ponds. The water may be cycled through the plant up to 17 times, going through the water purification technology between cycles.

Finally, another portion of the effluent is sent to the Granite Reef Recharge Project, where the water is allowed to percolate into the soil. The water that is released into the ground is of a grade that could be used in the city's water supply. Instead, it take a roundabout route through the aquifer. Unfortunately, the aquifers under Phoenix have been contaminated by industrial waste over the years and the City must treat the water once again before it can be used.

Tucson, located in Pima County, is taking a slightly different approach to traditional percolation. Like Phoenix, the county is allotted water from the Central Arizona Project (CAP) and the amount has proven to be above what the city currently requires. The utility director would not want to draw less than Pima County's allotment. Years earlier, Pima County dug a large borrow pit near Marana. The soil was used to build a series of dikes. City personnel viewed the borrow pit as an opportunity to allow the water from CAP to percolate into the aquifer as a deposit toward further withdrawals. The water released into the pit percolates down into the aquifer

Tucson has expanded much of its water storage capacity into the Avra Valley. This region has alluvial aquifers that allow water to percolate into the soil at a rate of three feet a day. The average rate of evaporation is around four percent which mean that most of the water sitting in ponds under the desert sun disappears into the ground faster than it can evaporate. Phoenix has now signed an agreement with Tucson to deposit one third of the water Phoenix receives from the CAP into the Tucson aquifers. In return, Phoenix received a portion of an aquifer further north.

I was a bit skeptical that water could just be poured into the aquifer and be available at some later date. I asked Julia Fonseca in Pima County if she thought this would be successful. Wasn't it possible that this water might just disappear along underground channels beyond the city's reach? She shrugged and simply replied, "We'll see."

In 2019, The Arizona Daily Star reported that water was flowing in the Santa Cruz once again on the Pima ancestral lands near San Xavier del Bac. With the addition of CAP water, the aquifer has indeed risen to a level where water is emerging into the channel. In one sense, this is a success as the river has returned. However, importing water from the Colorado River does not directly address the increasing demand on the aquifer.

As I consider the state of our aquifers, the image of the native man stooped over the trickle of water seeping from a rock face returns to me. Our arid land could support such a low demand. Today, as our population as expanded with large urban centers, the demand for water grows by leaps and bounds. We are not willing to return to the conservation-minded lifestyle of our the early settlers. If we are to be responsible with what water is available, we must curb our demand for the quantity we now use.

Arizona, being an arid state, has a long history of disputes over water rights, including the rights to large springs. There will come a day when despite stringent water restrictions, Arizona could face serious confrontation between aggrieved parties. We have already seen how in recent times, the disputes over water can lead to serious division in our communities. In the aftermath of the conflict between the City of Tombstone and the United States Forest Service, some of the people involved felt it was best to move away from Tombstone.

While researching this topic, I met a woman from a privately-held company who took a different approach to disputes over water policy. In the next chapter, I will consider our approach to disputes over water rights and what we value.

A Civilized Brawl

I recently stumbled across an old western on a cable channel. As the story concluded, the conflicting parties faced off in the street with pistols drawn. As our society has advanced, we understand that settling disputes at 20 paces with a six-shooter might not be the best approach to resolving disagreements over water rights.

Arizona separated from New Mexico and became an official territory under the auspices of the United States of America in 1866. Under the territorial government, residents began to formulate a legal code, including laws on water rights and usage. The legal code was further refined in the early 1900s as Arizona became forty-eighth state in our union.

By 1920, most of the surface water had been allocated. Forty years later, the federal government, through the Bureau of Reclamation, began to develop a system of dams to provide water for irrigation and regulate the available surface water.

In 1980, legislators became concerned that we were rapidly drawing down our water resources. The 1980 Groundwater Code became part of our legal code. Today, as we have become a litigious society, we are more likely to use the courts to settle our differences than pistols.

In studying Arizona's Legal Code, we find regulations for both surface water and ground water. We can visually observe and measure the amount of Arizona's surface water. The ground water is a bit more challenging. We cannot rely on our eyes and traditional methods of measurement to determine the amount of water we can safely use without endangering the cycle of regeneration. Instead, scientists rely on seismic tests and drill cores to determine the size of the aquifers below the surface of the ground.

As our population has grown, it has become apparent that our surface water is not limitless. Arizona's reliance on the Colorado River water for Maricopa, Pinal and Pima counties has been challenged as the climate affects the yield in the lower Colorado Basin. Most of our rivers are marked by dry stream beds throughout the year as the water is retained behind towering walls of cement. Seasons of drought excerbate conditions in our arid state.

Initially groundwater was considered our reserve if surface water should run

The Arizona Water Code & Arizona Springs

Traditionally, springs fall in a gray area between what is considered ground water and surface water. We find the springs under Title 45-141 in the Ariozna Legal Code:

> *The waters of all sources, flowing in streams, canyons, ravines or other natural channels, or in definite underground channels, whether perennial or intermittent, flood, waste or surplus water, and of lakes, ponds and springs on the surface, belong to the public and are subject to appropriation and beneficial use as provided in this chapter. (45-141)*
>
> *Public water will be judged on the basis, measure and limit to the use of water. (45-141)*

Since springs are considered to be public waters, a permit process is described as follows:

> *Any person, including the United States, the state or a municipality, intending to acquire the right to the beneficial use of water, shall make an application to the director of water resources for a permit to make an appropriation of the water. (45-152)*

Once a permit is obtained, the water must be used. Or the right to use the water may revert back to public domain:

> *Except as otherwise provided in this title or in title 48, when the owner of a right to the use of water ceases or fails to use the water appropriated for five successive years, the right to the use shall cease, and the water shall revert to the public and shall again be subject to appropriation. (45-141)*

dry. Now, we are drawing down our aquifers faster than they can be recharged. Many of the springs across southern Arizona and in the northeast and northwest corners of our state no longer produce water. Where once a well a hundred feet deep might provide water to a ranch family, today cities are drilling wells over a thousand feet deep.

In 1980, the legislature began wrestling with the issue of regulating ground water. Surface water rights govern the use of streams, rivers, lakes and reservoirs. In his analysis of the 1980 Water Code, John Lesky states, "Based on the premise that state government should, through the exercize of police power, directly control nearly every aspect of the developement, allocation and use of water in the major water-using areas of the state."

With the Groundwater Code, the legislature hoped to:

1) Control the severe draw down of ground water in the southern regions of our state.
2) Provide a blue print by which we allocated groundwater to meet the needs of our population as we grew.
3) To develop new water sources to augment the state's groundwater.

The law was intended to institute comprehensive groundwater conservation and management through the state. The state was divided into basins and sub-basins with the code stating that water could not be transferred from one basin to another. As an example, if Phoenix should find that it is outgrowing its supply of water, this urban center cannot transfer ground water from the Verde Valley to meet the demands of the residents in Phoenix.

After establishing the basins, the Code developed three levels of management.

1) In those areas with a low population and no irrigation, the code provided general guidelines that applied state-wide. Rural Water Groups have been formed in these regions to monitor and protect water resources.
2) The next level, Irrigation Non-Expansion Areas (INA), included areas with farming and industrial concerns that drew heavily on the water table. Irrigation might take place in the INAs but the region did not contain large irrigation districts. Three INAs are located around Douglas, Joseph City and the Harquehala Valley.
3) The largest urban and farming centers were placed in a category for Active Management Areas (AMA). There are five AMAs in the state centered around Pinal County, Santa Cruz County and Prescott, Phoenix, and Tucson.

Statewide provisions were instated to slow the process of stripping the aquifers of water. Of these, four have left a distinct footprint on the state. One provision ruled that previously un-irrigated land could not be farmed with irrigation in the future. This meant that if land was withdrawn from irrigation, it could not be returned later to the status of irrigated farm land. As the citrus orchards and fields disappeared from the Valley of the Sun, the land was transformed into housing subdivisions. Even if there was a desire to return to agrarian development in the region, this land cannot be irrigated as it was in the 1950s when the desert became the citrus capital of the nation.

Another provision required new industry in the state to apply for a permit to use groundwater for industrial purposes. Restrictions were placed on drilling of new wells with a large diameter. Finally, the state now requires new subdivisions to show they have a hundred-year supply of water that is consistent with the goals of the state. One of the results of these provisions has been the widespread use of rock in natural landscaping in new subdivisions.

One concern that has not been actively addressed is the overlapping of claims on the large aquifers. A subdivision such as the one at Bellemont, may claim water from the C-aquifer while Flagstaff, 10 miles east, may also claim water from the C-aquifer. The C-aquifer is showing signs of drying from the west. The well fields for Flagstaff are briskly pulling water out of the aquifer on Bellemont's eastern exposure. Flagstaff returns a portion of their effluent to the aquifer but this does not raise the level of the aquifer near Bellemont. If the drought does not lift, in time the 100-year supply for Bellemont may fall short. Across the state a number of towns and counties may well feel the pinch in time, providing ample ground for legal action.

Rural Water Groups

Cobre Valley Water Partnership
Coconino Plateau Watershed Partnership
Fort Huachuca Sentinel Landscape
    Restoration Partnership
Friends of Verde River
Gila Watershed Partnership
Little Colorado River Watershed
    Coordinating Council
Mohave County Water Authority
Northern Arizona Municipal Water
    Users Association
Oak Creek Watershed Council
Upper Agua Fria Watershed Council
Upper San Pedro Partnership

In southern Arizona, the AMAs may have been a good attempt toward conserving water, however, in some areas, the growth rate is unsustainable. As I noted earlier, the water table in Sulphur Springs Valley has dropped over 200 feet. In the San Pedro River watershed, subdivisions are rapidly multiplying. Homes now spread throughout the area around Sierra Vista and Hereford while the military base has also grown. Both the Sulphur Springs Valley and San Pedro River Valley are not included in an AMA. In the last few years, the bickering over water has intensified. Further action may be required to protect what resources we have left.

Ultimately, the goal of the 1980 Groundwater Code is to achieve a level of withdrawal statewide that equals the level of recharge. In the previous chapter, I discussed the efforts by several urban centers to recycle effluent and storm runoff into deep wells that allow the water to percolate into the aquifers.

An encouraging note: The San Pedro has seen an improvement as agreements have been put in place to increase the amount of water flowing along the riverbed. When I dropped into the streambed off State Route 90 in 2018, I was pleasantly surprised to find the channel filled with the water stretching from bank to bank.

When we examine the amount of water that we are removing from the aquifers versus the amount returned, we are still falling short. The springs of southern Arizona are witness to that shortfall. Effectively educating our residents in the conservation of water would help. This must be a much stronger, aggressive effort than school children drawing picture of ways to save water. Usage rates on our water bills coupled with a strong campaign to link each daily task to the amount of water used might be a good tool. Pairing this with punitive rates for overdraws on the water table would increase the public's urgency in conserving water.

On a community wide level, we may need to reduce the number of private pools, making public pools popular again. Water will no longer be so frequently used in desert landscaping on the corporate level. We must place an emphasis on both the minute and the greater use.

On a state-wide level, we may need to revisit our approach to the AMA and INA regulations. The water requirements in urban regions are very different from those in the rural counties. The state is now on its fifth revision of the 1980 Water Management Plan.

One person I interviewed compared the rural counties to the wild west where anything goes. She stated that a permit to drill a new well is more of an adminstrative matter than a calculation over whether the water is available for the new homes in accordance with other stakeholders in the region.

This source believed the Arizona Department of Water Resources should require more people in the field working with water departments and landowners. There is a gap between the knowledge of those serving short term in our our legislature and the long term knowlege of those who work in the field. We need more cooperation between those who make the regulation and those who understand what is available and what is at stake.

Like many others, I hate the idea of further government regulation in our private lives. But at some point, the people of Arizona will have to discuss what we value and what we are willing to sacrifice to maintain a reasonable standard of living.

There is another approach, one might say a gentler approach, that is worth considering along with the legislative and legal restrictions to help balance demand and resolve disputes over water.

Dr. Kira Artemis Russo became interested in Native American water rights as a graduate student in Sacramento, California under the tuteledge of a professor of Sioux heritage. The history of the abuse of native American rights has long been documented, with a poor record of remediation.

Dr.. Russo suggests that we think about what we value when we consider water usage. As she wrote her dissertation, she found that asking what we value and how we use water sometimes led to very different approaches on water issues.

Out of her dual interest in water issues and the dialogue of the public square, she founded a consulting firm that helps communities examine the question of what the residents value as they seek to form a policy for water use.

As she enters a community, her first concern is to develop a sense of trust with each of the stakeholders involved with the water use within the region or community. Historically, trust has been in short supply when people's lives are at risk. Each of us wants to protect what we have and what we perceive as needed in the future. Dr. Russo notes that some of the conflicts over water rights date back one hundred years or more. That sense of trust, of shared value, was never developed between the parties involved.

The first instinct when seeking community consensus is to gather people together for one large meeting where all will express their concern. How many times have such meetings devolved into shouting matches, with some complaining that they were not allowed to fully express their concern?

Dr. Russo initially chooses to meet with each stakeholder individually, one on one. As that individual talks about the issue and their concerns, she carefully takes notes on what is said. She places an asterick next to phrases and words that are repeated, knowing these expressions may indicate deeply held concerns. She asks each individual about their water use and how they value water. I suspect if we each took the time to consider that question we might be surprised at what comes to the surface in our answers.

After talking to each stakeholder, she compiles the information she has received, looking for common ground. Where do all the parties agree? In our deeply divided society, I think we can say that agreement is often in short supply.

The next question is to consider the stakeholders and who might be willing to work together to find a common solution to even one small problem. She believes that if she can find one small area where people can work together for a solution, she has made a beginning toward establishing trust. Out of that beginning, may come further agreement. If no agreement develops, the deeply divided parties may look back with fond memories on a time they did work together.

This seems like a small thing: to find common ground, no matter how small or big that moment of kinship may be. Trust is nourished as we begin to see another person sharing a common value. The political arena of past years has given us a number of examples of men who bitterly disagreed on almost every subject and yet were able to move forward on legislation over an issue they found in common.

Once an area of mutual benefit and common achievement has been established, small communities have often found the value of working as a one entity rather than individually. As an example, many of the small towns in northern Arizona find they are separated from each other by long stretches of open land. With a common need for water, these communities might find it beneficial to work together, finding solutions and inspiring each other toward new initiatives. For example, communities might choose to order equipment together. Cooperation could also be the basis of an aggressive campaign toward reducing the amount of water pulled from the ground and building facilities to treat affluent.

The alternative would be communities vying for precious resources, suspicious of every move others make in their region. The goal of cooperation is part of the initiative behind the Coconino Plateau Water Advisory Council which brings together all the stakeholders in northern Arizona who rely on the high country aquifers. Their meetings are one of cooperation and mutually shared information rather than adversity.

As Dr. Russo wraps up her interaction with a community, she brings the stakeholders together to compare their responses. She identifies how many stakeholders are interested in the issue that first brought her to the community and how many are willing to work toward a solution.

She might ask what issues the stakeholders find beyond those she has identified. She may discuss what each party expects from the other. And finally, she asks the participants what issues require further work beyond what has been accomplished.

While this may all sound theoretical, Dr. Russo acknowledges that there are some disagreements that will not find common ground. These are the disputes that end up in court. She is not a big fan of settling issues through the courts as such action often leaves one party the winner and the other the loser.

"If each side will move just a little . . ." And she smiles. Is that not the optimism of a negotiator?

We seek common ground.

From Need to Nurture

So what do we value? Can the springs of Arizona find a champion?

It is time to reconsider what we value when we think of water in a desert land. Like the hermit of Sycamore Canyon, do we need to stop, to consider what we doing and to make a U-turn? Do we need to discipline our culture, moving from an emphasis on what we need to what we can nurture? Can we change how we live to preserve this natural resource?

Arizona's springs are more than just water leaking from the ground. Springs speak of life down to the level of atoms, to invertebrates almost invisible to the human eye. If we choose to ignore the most basic forms of life, we threaten our own. Springs carry the promise of life, of verdant abundance overflowing into deep pools of water that refresh, that restore life.

The canary is singing.

~ Citizen Science ~

WHAT ARE THE FACTORS IN CLASSIFYING A SPRING?

1) Out of what type of rock does the aquifer emerge?
2) What is the environment in which the spring emerges?
3) What is the geomorphology of the spring orifice?
4) What is the appearance as the spring discharges?
5) Is there a spring channel and how is it formed?
6) How does the water flow from the orifice? Does it vary?
7) Can you check the water temperature?
8) If you have a home laboratory, can you determine what mineral elements are present?
9) Is there anything that indicate the spring may be polluted?
10) Use a small kit off the internet, check the pH on the spring. What is the alkaline level?
10) Can you test for dissolved solids? Is there evidence of travertine build-up around the spring?
11) What is the average air temperature around the spring? Is subject to change with the seasons?
12) What is the average rainfall in the are around the spring?
13) Is the growing season year-round or inhibited by cold temperatures?
14) Are there other springs nearby?
15) Can you identify more than one habitat within the riparian zone?
16) Look a little closer. Waht kind of diversity can you see within the riparian zone around the spring?
17) Name some of the species that have visited the spring - this means check for insect life and the prints of warm-blooded mammals.
18) What is the land use around the spring? Has the water from the spring been put to another use?
19) Take a photo of the spring and habitat. Upload the photo with your information to Citizen Science.gov.

~ Springs Stewardship Institute

If water begins to bubble up in your yard where water has never appeared before, assume you have a broken pipe. There's a good chance this is not a spring!

Springs Appearing in The Desert's Draught

Agua Caliente
Alamo
Alpine
Apache
Arizona
Babes Hole
Bathtub
Bear
Bearpaw
Big (North Rim)
Big (Pinetop-Lakeside)
Blue
Bog
Carr
Castle
Castle (Hot)
Cave
Clark (Flagstaff)
Clark (Huachuca)
Cliff
Clifton
Dorsey
Dow
Dragoon
Flagstaff
Fossil
General
Gilliard
Guevavi
Hooker
Horton
Hospital
Hoxworth
Indian (Eden)
Jack Smith
Jacobs Well
Kelsey
La Cebadilla
Laws
Las Cienegas
LO
McMillan
Mangum
Miller
Moencopi Wash
Monkey
Montezuma Well
Mountain Sheep
Navajo
Old Town
O'Leary
O'Neil
Pakoon
Philomena
Pipe
Pivot Rock
Pomeroy Tanks
Quartzite
Quitobaquito
Ramsey
Raspberry
Ringbolt
Roaring
Rucker Canyon
Russell?
Sawmill
Sipapu
Snowslide
Slaughter's Ranch
Sowats
Spitz
Sterling
Three Forks
Thunder River
Tunnel
Turkey Tank
Veit
Ventana
Warm
White Rock
Mangum
Miller
Moencopi Wash
Monkey
Montezuma Well
Mountain Sheep
Navajo
Old Town
O'Leary
O'Neil
Pakoon
Philomena
Pipe
Pivot Rock
Pomeroy Tanks
Quartzite
Quitobaquito
Ramsey
Raspberry
Ringbolt
Roaring
Rucker Canyon
Russell?
Sawmill
Sipapu
Snowslide
Slaughter's Ranch
Sowats
Spitz
Sterling
Three Forks
Thunder River
Tunnel
Turkey Tank
Veit
Ventana
Warm
White Rock

Acknowledgments

For years, I had come across springs as I hiked throughout Arizona. When I began researching the springs of Arizona, I arrived at the Springs Stewardship Institute at the Museum of Northern Arizona. Thank you Jeri, Larry and your staff for the work your have done over the years in cataloging and preserving the springs. Most of all, thank you for your generosity in sharing what you know!

Thank you to Samanatha 'Sami' Hammer, with the Sky Island Alliance, for a listening ear and quiet comments.

Joan Baker, thank you for your encouragement and help with research. Dan & Debbie Cook, thank you for your help with Babbit Spring. It is sad that we can no longer reveal those places we treasure due to the vandalism that takes place.

Julia Fontaine, thank you for the discussion that gave me so much to consider and your enthusiasm in the topic, for your encouragement to go forward!

I have to mention the faithfulness of my husband as we traveled throughout the state - he hates traveling - but he loves me! Thank you!

And to Tim East with your wife, Kathy, thank you for saving my life!

There are so many I interviewed and will forget to mention - please know that each one of you had a role in forming this manuscript.

To the men and women who meet faithfully to discuss water issues on the Coconino Plateau, especially Ron Doba, Jon Martinez and Erin Young. Thank you for allowing me to listen and learn!

To Shannon and Karen Clark for their knowledge of the springs and oversight of the manuscript.

To the many public officials I interviewed who gave me their time and insight. Thank you to each of you.

For Katie, thank you for your editing and insight.

Thank you to those who walk miles with me: Nancy, Kathy, Serenity, Gavin, Sutton, Lexi, Ken and others. To each of you, may the journey be more pleasant.

Bibliography

A Guide to the Beale Wagon Road through the Coconino National Forest, Jack Smith, TofB Publishing, 1991

Desert River Crossing: Historic Lee's Ferry on the Colorado River, W.L. Rusho and C. Gregory Crampton, Peregrine Smith, Inc. 1975

Disaster at the Colorado, Charles W. Baley, Utah State University Press, 2002

John Udell, The Rest of the Story: With an Adventure on the Beale Wagon Road, Jack Smith, Tales of the Beale Road Publishing Co.

Missouri 49er: The Journal of Willian W. Hunter on the Southern Gold trail, Edited by David P Robrock, University of New Mexico, 1992

Paahu (Water) and Hopi Traditions, Thesis written by Kristian A. Diaz, University of Colorado/ Boulder, 2011

Oral history of the Yavapai, Mike Harrison & John Williams, with Sigrid Khera, Edited by Carolina Butler, Acacia Publishing, 2012

They Came to the Mountain, Platt Cline, Northland Publishing, 1998

On the Border with Crook, John G. Bourke, Sky Horse Publishing, 2014

Springs and Wells, USDA Nat'l Resources Conservation Service, Chapter 11, 2012

Articles:
Post Monument Fire Floods and Debris Flow in the Huachuca Mountains, Ann Youberg and Phil Pearthree, Arizona Geology Magazine, Sept 12, 2011

Radioactive Water Near Hopi Springs, Arizona Daily Sun, Cyndy Cole, March 17, 2007

Showdown at the H2O Corral, CNN, May 10, 2012; Multiple Media
    Reports on Lawsuit between Tombstone and the US Forest Service

A guide to the Geology of the Santa Catalina Mountains, Arizona: The Geology and Life Zone of a Madrean Sky Island, John Bezy, Arizona
    Geological Survey, 2016

Ancient aquifers are dropping as Tucson's suburbs pump groundwater, Tony Davis, Tucson.com, Feb 29, 2020

Arizona's Legendary Hot Springs, Vince Murray, True West Magazine 2018

Websites:
San Jose de Sonoita Grant by J.J. Bowden, The New Mexico Office of the State Historian

https://archive.epa.gov/region9/superfund/web/pdf/tubacity-smlopez-hopiwaterresources.pdf

https://www.empireranchfoundation.org/empire-ranch/establishment-of-the-empire-ranch-a-chronology

ArizonaStateParks.Com - Historic Trails of Arizona

https://maps.ngdc.noaa.gov/viewers/hot_springs

https://new.azwater.gov/sites/default/files/media/Arizona%20Groundwater_Code_1.pdf

Reports:
Archaeological Investigations and Data Recovery at Historic Block 83, Tucson, Edited by J. Homer Thiel, Arizona Desert Archeology Inc, 2009

Post-Monument Fire Floods and Debris Flows in the Huachuca Mountains, Southern Arizona, Ann Youberg & Phil Pearthree, Arizona Geology Magazine, 2011

Desert Basins of the Southwest, S.A. Leake, A.D. Konieczki, J.A.H. Rees, USGS, 2000

Report on Geo-thermal potential - http://repository.azgs.az.gov/sites/default/files/dlio/files/nid1579/ofr-14-06_azhotspringsv1_0.pdf

USGS Arizona's Santa Cruz River Chronicled in New Environmental History, August 13, 2014

Geohydrology and Water Use in the Southern Apache County, Larry Mann - USGS and E.A. Memecek - ADWR, 1983

Thermal Springs of Arizona, James Witcher, Fieldnotes, AzGS 1981

https://www.nps.gov/hosp/learn/education/upload/followthewater

Final Hydrographic Survey Report for Hopi Indians Reservation in General Adjudication of Little Colorado River System, Arizona Department of Water Resources, December 2015

Geology and Water Resources of the Sulphur Springs Valley, Arizona, O.E. Meinzer and F.C. Kelton, USGS, 1913

Environmental Assessment San Bernardino National Wildlife Refige Well 10, Nuclear Regulastory Commission, J.T. Ensminger, C.E. Easterly, R.H. Ketelle, H. Quarles, M.C. Wade, September 1999

Geology and Geomorphology of the Southwestern Moenkopi Plateau and Southern Ward Terrace, Arizona, by G.H. Billingsley, USGS, 1983

Arizona Geological Report on Clifton Hot Springs, Arizona, by David E. Brown, Arizona Geological Survey

Geothermal Resource Evaluation at Castle Hot Springs, Arizona, by Michael Sheridan, Richard Satkin and Kenneth Wohletz, Arizona Geological Survey, 1980

An Investigation of Thermal Springs Throughout Arizona: Geochemical, Isotopic, Geological Characterizaton, Arizona Basin and Range Province, by Diane Love, Brian Gootee, Joseph Cook, Michael Mahan and Jon Spencer, Arizona Geological Survey, 2014

Hydrogeology and Sources of Water to Select Springs in Black Canyon,
South of Hoover Dam, Lake Mead National Recreation Area, Nevada and Arizona, By Michael J. Moran, Jon W. Wilson, and L. Sue Beard, NPS and USGS, 2015

A Guide to the Geology of the Flagstaff Area, John V. Bezy, Arizona Geological Survey, 2003

Geohydrology and the Effects of Water Use in the Black Mesa area and On the Navajo and Hopi Reservations, James H. Eychaner, USGS, 1983

A Guide to the Geology of the Sedona and Oak Creek Canyon Areas, Arizona, John Bezy, Arizona Geological Society, 2012

A Conceptual Hydrogeologic model for Fossil Springs, Western Mogollonn Rim, Arizona: Implications for Regional Springs Processes, Megan Green, Northern Arizona University, 2008

Restoration Benefits to Natural Springs in the Lake Mary Watershed,
Clairesse Nash and Aregai Tecle and Ashley Craig, School of Forestry, Northern Arizona University, 2015

Irrigation Districts in a Changing West: an Overview, John Lesky, Volume 1982, #1, Arizona Statutes Legal Review

www.ingramcontent.com/pod-product-compliance
Lightning Source LLC
Chambersburg PA
CBHW061153010526
44118CB00027B/2958